WHAT PEOPLE ARE SAYING ABOUT
do less, be more

John Busacker weaves together inspiring, personal stories with practical success principles that give hope and courage to pursue one's values. ***Do less, be more*** is a compelling call to live a focused and generous life that makes a difference.

—JONATHAN T.M. RECKFORD, CEO, Habitat for Humanity International

Within each of us there is a unique life story which is meant to be told. Will we accept the lead role for our own lives or play a bit part? The answer lies in one's focus. ***Do less, be more*** offers a **transformative script** for anyone seeking their own potential.

—JAY BENNETT, Vice Chairman, National Christian Foundation

This is **the right message for the present age.** Everywhere I go around the world I see the results of disengagement: Leaders direct without passion, and employees struggle to define a real rationale for too much of too much. John's message is clear, and his story offers examples of the choices we can make to live richer, more productive, more meaningful lives.

—PETER GEREND, Regional Managing Director, Duke Corporate Education

The simple elegance of *doing less* and *being more* has taught me that "**enough is as good as a feast.**"

—PHILIP STYRLUND, CEO, The Summit Group

Getting caught in the web of "doing" can disorient and disconnect us from finding any deep satisfaction, despite our best efforts and intentions. John Busacker's book is **a guide out of this web of autopilot activity** and into the riveting clarity of a focused life.

—BOB MANN, Former Vice President, Cargill Ferrous International

This wise, compassionate book is grounded in refreshing new ways to **overcome our hurry-sickness** and filled with engaging practices to recapture the good life—for good.

—RICHARD LEIDER, Best-selling author of *Repacking Your Bags, The Power of Purpose* and *Life Reimagined*

In a time-wearied world that buys the lie that busier is better, John Busacker offers **a countercultural call to *drop the ball* and reclaim your uniqueness and time**, becoming *fully engaged* in the only life you'll ever have.

—DR. MIKE GIBSON, Lead Pastor, Christ Lutheran Church and School, Costa Mesa, CA

Why am I here? Dig deeply into *do less, be more* and the answers will appear. You can live an **inspired life of meaning and purpose**. What more could you ask?

—DAVID MCNALLY, CEO, TransForm Corporation & Author:
  Even Eagles Need a Push

Living *fully engaged* is far more art than science, and John has a unique gift for nurturing this along through simple-yet-profound awarenesses and practices that literally transform how we live. *Doing less* and *being more* has **helped me move beyond the surface of things to find greater significance and deeper fulfillment in my everyday life.**

—KRISTIN EVENSON, Managing Director, Nonprofit Solutions,
  Integrated Governance Solutions (IGS)

Relief and hope are just two of the emotions I felt as I took to heart the words in this book. More does not lead to a more fulfilling life; it only leads to a fuller one. That truth seems so obvious, but so often I end up missing it. Thank you, John, for getting my attention and helping me take some **steps toward living a clearer, simpler, and more meaningful life.**

—DR. SCOTT RISCHE, Executive Director, PLI-International

John has "softened the soul" of our organization with his principles of a focused life. The result has been **explosive growth with a deep sense of purpose and satisfaction.**

—JOEL A. JOHNSON, Managing Partner, Thrivent Financial

We committed to growing *fully engaged* members and employees as core success measures. What a difference it has made! John's **straightforward insight and wisdom** in *do less, be more* have guided and inspired us to stay on track with the importance of "being more."

—BRAD L. HEWITT, President and CEO, Thrivent Financial

Do less, be more hits the mark for helping people successfully navigate in the increasingly complex world we now live in. I have found it has an **awesome return on investment** for individuals and organizations who desire to become all that they can be.

—JIM LEIGHTON, President, Perdue Foods and author of *Getting FIT—Unleashing the Power of Fully Integrated Teams,* Founder of The Get FIT Movement

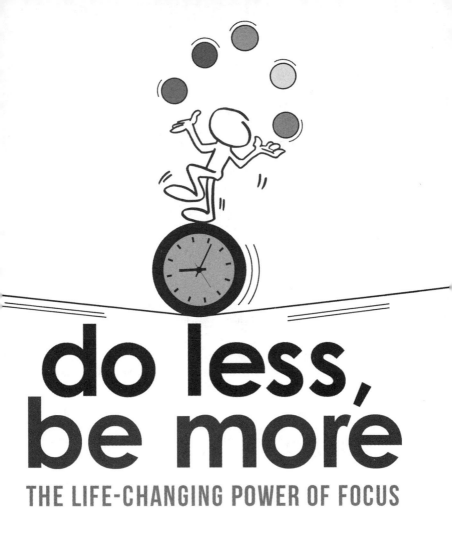

do less, be more

THE LIFE-CHANGING POWER OF FOCUS

do less, be more
© 2013 by John Busacker

ISBN 978-1-60587-526-2

Published by Freeman-Smith, a division of Worthy Media, Inc.,
134 Franklin Road, Suite 200, Brentwood, Tennessee 37027.

The quoted ideas expressed in this book (but not Scripture verses) are not, in all cases, exact quotations, as some have been edited for clarity and brevity. In all cases, the author has attempted to maintain the speaker's original intent. In some cases, quoted material for this book was obtained from secondary sources, primarily print media. While every effort was made to ensure the accuracy of these sources, the accuracy cannot be guaranteed. For additions, deletions, corrections, or clarifications in future editions of this text, please write Freeman-Smith.

All Scripture quotations, unless otherwise noted, are taken from:

The Message. Copyright © 1993, 1994, 1995, 1996, 2000, 2001, 2002 by Eugene Peterson. Used by permission of NavPress, Colorado Springs, CO. All rights reserved.

Scripture quotations marked NIV are taken from the HOLY BIBLE, NEW INTERNATIONAL VERSION*. NIV*. Copyright © 1973, 1978, 1984 by Biblica, Inc™. Used by permission. All rights reserved worldwide.

Cover Design by Kim Russell / Wahoo Designs
Page Layout by Bart Dawson

Printed in the United States of America

1 2 3 4 5—SBI—17 16 15 14 13

do less,
be more

THE LIFE-CHANGING POWER OF FOCUS

FREEMAN-SMITH

JOHN BUSACKER

. . . .

TO CAROL

My best friend, soul mate,
and unwavering inspiration
to *do less* and *be more*

. . . .

How Focused Are You?

Take this quick quiz to find out.

On a scale of 1–10 (1 being not at all; 10 being completely satisfied), how would you rate yourself in these six important areas of life?

_8_ I have a deep sense of purpose. I know where I'm going in life and why I do what I do.

_1_ My current physical routines increase my energy and personal resilience.

_5_ I am authentically optimistic even in the midst of bad news and life's daily struggles.

_8_ I fully use both sides of my brain—analytical and creative.

_1_ I take time for intimate relationships with friends and family members. They are a priority.

_8_ I am working in an area of my passions and strengths.

Contents

AWARENESS
Are you living purposefully?

ALIGNMENT
*How does what you have and what you
do match what you really want out of life?*

From Average to Astonishing By Doing *Less*!

Really live each day—and love it!

I knew my wife, Carol, and I were in for a long haul even before our boys started elementary school. Carol was talking with our neighbors in Seattle, Washington, and was blown away to learn that they were "double-booking" their children in kindergarten.

I knew the airlines regularly did this—and they still do—but *kindergarten*?

Our neighbors' actions weren't driven by the fear of not getting a seat, but rather by the primal desire to get a "jump on first grade." So the little neighbor boys and girls were enrolled in one school for the morning and another for the afternoon session.

Now I fully acknowledge that we live in a hyper-competitive era driven in part by what best-selling author Thomas Friedman calls a "flat world." Don't get me wrong. Education is vital. But this incessant and ever-increasing gravitational pull for being more, doing more, and having more—beginning in the very earliest stages of life—is wearing people out. It wore us out. And I bet you're reading this book because it's wearing you out too.

In the end, living and working in double-booked mode leads to sleepwalking exhausted through your waking hours. How can you enjoy the beauty that each new day can bring if you're feeling overstressed and numb? Or if you're so bored with the way your life is going that you miss the energy and vitality your day could have? Or if you're feeling hopeless that things will never change for the better?

Double-booking doesn't create a *focused* life. In fact, it does just the opposite. It amounts to an "air guitar life"—furious motion and considerable energy, but in the end no sound and little lasting impact.

I want you to ask yourself one question: "What should I do with my life?"

If you responded, "Exactly what I'm doing right now," then congratulations! You are among the 1 percent of the population of people who don't need this book.

You know where you are in all areas of life, you are satisfied with where you're going, fulfilled by what you're doing, and heading straight-as-an-arrow down the life path to where you want to be in the future. You are *focused* and living the life you were designed to live. So pass this book to a friend or colleague.

Double-booking amounts to an "air guitar life"—furious motion and considerable energy but in the end no sound and little lasting impact.

But if you're in the 99 percent majority, like most people who feel that a key ingredient is missing in their level of satisfaction and fulfillment in one or more areas, then *do less, be more* is perfect for you.

If one or several of the questions in the "How Focused Are You?" quiz caused you to pause and reflect, and perhaps feel a little lost and nervous, *do less, be more* can help.

Here's a litmus test of whether you are *truly focused*.

Quick—what's your first thought when the alarm goes off in the morning?

Are you feeling **burned out**—fatigued by family obligations and buried under the burden of work? Before your feet even hit the floor, do you feel defeated by deadlines and worn down by the worry of keeping all of the balls in the air? Are your family, fitness, finances, or faith on tilt?

Or are you feeling **rusted out**—merely marking time in your relationships, spiritual life, and work? Do you put life on hold until "someday"—the weekend, vacation, or retirement? Have you put your passion on pause and dug your routines into a rut?

You were not designed to live this way! You have gifts to give, family to love, and dreams to live. You were created to learn and grow, not to replicate and repeat. What if you could not only live each day, but *really* live it—and love it?

You have gifts to give, family to love, and dreams to live. You were created to learn and grow, not to replicate and repeat.

When was the last time you felt truly focused?

Perhaps you were riveted by a project at **work** because it tapped into your unique giftedness and you knew in your bones that it would touch someone's life in a meaningful way or deliver lasting value to the planet.

Or maybe you felt fully alive in a **relationship.** You had the deep sense of being completely in tune with the person you love the most. So much so that the unspoken communication resonated louder than any words either of you could have spoken to each other.

Maybe you were gripped in your **faith** with an overwhelming sense of God's presence and love that brought deep joy and an inexplicable peace of heart and boldness of action.

We all deeply long to be this engaged—to feel connected, joyful, and alive. The question is, how do you lead an engaged *life,* rather than simply stringing together fleeting *moments* of passion?

|ful•ly en•gaged|

To be riveted.
To be fully alive.
To be gripped.

Take a close look at each of these three descriptions of full engagement. The common denominator in each is *time.* It takes time to be *riveted, fully alive, gripped.* Full engagement is not characterized as much by its pace as by its presence. The core of each description is not *doing* something, but *being* someone—the person you are designed to be with your unique passion, gifts, vision, life experiences, and relationships.

We all long to feel called, connected, and fully committed. We all want to know that what we do in life has lasting value.

Here's the key: You need to **DO *less*** in order to **BE *more.*** To live this way is completely countercultural, especially in America, the nation of exhausted doers. It's so tempting to think:

- *If 50 hours of work gets me in the queue for the next promotion, 65 hours will only accelerate the process.*

- *If my best friend is a room mom, I should be one too.*

- *If practicing sports for two hours a day is good, three hours a day year-round will help fashion my child into the next great pro athlete.*
- *If church on Sundays is good, additional Wednesday night Bible study and Friday morning small groups will surely make me more spiritual.*

And it's all a lie! The end result is exhaustion, not engagement.

This book takes a bold stand on what it takes to live a focused life. It is both *personal* and *practical.*

Personal, because you'll be blessed to walk closely with people who don't have it all figured out but are intentional about doing less and being more while living out their days with purpose and passion.

Practical, because each chapter concludes with simple practices that are a catalyst for deeper conversation and bolder action, all in the pursuit of a *focused* life.

Erwin Raphael McManus, a native of El Salvador, well-known speaker and Christian thinker, and pastor of a large church in Los Angeles, California, was once challenged by his daughter to choose his words carefully when he spoke at an event. "Remember, nothing less than *astonishing*!" she told him.

What if *you* felt summoned every day to that same level of focus? What if you lived each moment as if it were "nothing less than astonishing"?

God uses ordinary people like you and me to do astonishing things if, and only if, we are *truly focused.*

It's time to live in a way that makes good on all the talents and promise you were born with—and to enjoy the satisfaction, success, and excitement that come as a result.

Adventure awaits.

Let's be astonished together. Let's DO *less* and BE *more.*

All you have to do is turn the page.

AWARENESS

Are you living purposefully?

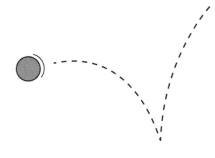

CHAPTER ONE

Measure Your Worth

Your life is worth so much more than money.

It seemed like a good plan at the time.

Seven years ago, our family decided to spend spring break in Tanzania, East Africa. One night, we stayed in a quaint African lodge on the edge of the Serengeti Plain. The plan was to wake up at dawn, drive out into the vast national park at first light, and see who was eating whom for breakfast. By noon, we were to have made it to the gate of the Ngorongoro Crater, intending to venture down in it for additional afternoon wildlife viewing.

Of course, nothing on an African safari goes exactly according to plan. It rained during the night, so what passes for roads quickly transformed to goo-filled ruts. Our guide, Moses, was forced to navigate by feel, having neither a map nor GPS.

It became increasingly clear that we were driving in circles, making no progress toward the Ngorongoro Crater. Not wanting to sound any alarms, as discreetly as I could, I leaned forward and quietly inquired, "Moses, are we lost?"

What followed was a rapid-fire conversation between Moses and Ramos, our driver. Having limited Swahili vocabulary but reading the body language and urgency of tone, I was guessing that this was not good news!

After about a minute, Moses leaned back, looked straight at Carol, and delivered the verdict: "We *could* be."

Uh-oh!

Carol, who is an intensive-care nurse by background and who values both having and then executing an orderly plan, began to envision our imminent death at the mouths of the same lions we had just observed eating a Grant's gazelle for breakfast.

I knew what our older son, Brett, was thinking by the gleam in his eye. He who has never seen a 50-foot cliff he didn't want to drop on a snowboard and who authentically values adventure, especially accompanied by a little danger, was thinking, *This is AWESOME! I'm the fastest guy in the car! So what do I have to worry about anyway?*

Humans, it is said, are the only animals that speed up when lost. This is especially true of American humans.

Moses, our guide, did the exact opposite. Rather than speed up, he came to a complete stop and waited for someone else to catch up so he could determine where we were in the Serengeti and then chart a new course to our destination.

He stopped **DO**-ing in order to focus on **BE**-ing found.

What we needed that day on the Serengeti Plain was a GPS. What an amazing technological device. Using the broad perspective of three coordinates—latitude, longitude, and altitude—a GPS can find your car amongst the millions of cars on the planet, tell you exactly where you are, and then help you navigate to your desired destination…all in a soothing, patient voice, too.

When you screw up or are too stubborn to heed its advice, it doesn't bark, "You moron! Why don't you ever listen?"

No, it simply says, "Recalculating," and calmly charts and then gives you a new route. Now that's grace!

So why don't we apply the same broad perspective and grace to our own lives? Our tendency is to zero in on only one coordinate—money—and then ratchet up our speed at all costs to get more money or the stuff that more money can buy (like prestige or power).

Let's be honest. Too often we value our stuff above our health, relationships, spiritual vitality, or life itself, don't we? If you don't think so, take a quick peek at your schedule right now…bet you just winced a bit, didn't you?

Humans, it is said, are the only animals that speed up when lost. This is especially true of American humans.

It's so easy for our personal GPS to get messed up—especially if we're willing to let a single-minded pursuit of financial assets spin us in circles in the wilderness. After all, we believe assets and liabilities determine our financial health and overall success…don't they?

Net worth—what you have minus what you owe—has long been the key scorecard of prosperity and progress. Are you successful? On track? Check your *net worth* statement.

But is that *really* an accurate measure of a successful, *fully engaged* life?

An abundant life is that healthy but elusive blend of play, work, friendship, family, money, spiritual growth, and contribution.

Abundance creates contentment. Contentment inspires gratitude. Your peace of mind, sense of fulfillment, and joy are determined by how well you manage *many* life dimensions, not just your finances. Intimate relationships, deep spiritual life, right work, good health, a vibrant community, interesting hobbies, and active learning all impact your sense of engagement with life.

Life worth is the investment you make into and the return you receive from all of these dimensions. It is both internal (a deep personal sense of engagement and fulfillment) and external (the ability to bring joy and lasting value to others). And, like a GPS, it takes more than one coordinate to determine your location and direction.

You can be *fully engaged* with little or no *net worth*. Here's what I mean.

Net worth: what you have minus what you owe.

Life worth: the investment you make into and the return you receive from all life dimensions.

The first time I visited Tanzania, I was amazed at how content the people seemed to be, even though they had next to nothing in possessions. I wondered, *Is it because they are unencumbered by the shackles of "stuff" that they are fully able to connect with their families and friends? Is that why they are happily able to do the work required to live yet another day? Why they are content, even when they're not sure sometimes where their next meal is coming from?*

Upon further reflection, I couldn't help but add to these thoughts: *And why is this sense of joy sorely lacking in our affluent Western world?*

The thought was sobering…and enlightening.

As Os Guinness says:

The trouble is that, as modern people, we have too much to live *with,* and too little to live *for.* In the midst of material plenty, we have spiritual poverty.[1]

Simply stated, material wealth is measured by *net worth*. Spiritual wealth and engagement are summed up by *life worth*. So let me ask you: What's your *life worth* right now?

Many people decide they must build their *net worth* first in order to fund *life worth* later.

But putting life on hold for one more business deal, one more project, a pay increase, a hopeful inheritance upon a relative's death, or an investment return ensnares the unsuspecting in its grip of "not quite enough." It can slowly form habits of overwork and selfishness. The focal point is always on what's *next* instead of what's *first.*

Do you find yourself falling into the trap of thinking, *Hey, I'll just hang in there. What's coming next has got to be better.*

If so, you are in danger of driving in endless circles—and exhausting yourself in the process.

Don't fall for that kind of thinking. Dreams delayed can become a life unlived. As American journalist and bestselling author Po Bronson put it:

It turns out that having the financial independence to walk away rarely triggers people to do just that. The reality is, making money is such hard work that it changes you. It takes twice as long as anyone plans for. It requires more sacrifice than anyone expects. You become so emotionally invested in that world—and psychologically adapted to it—that you don't really want to ditch it.[2]

Dreams delayed can become a life unlived.

Always **DO**-ing *more* ultimately causes us to **BE** *less*—less of a friend, mother, partner, student, or son.

I know. I've experienced it firsthand. I spent 14 years in the financial services industry, sitting at the table with countless people as they discussed their life dreams and financial goals.

What moved me were the life stories of the people with whom I met. Embedded in the discussion of money were the hopes, dreams, fears, regrets, beliefs, and biases of each person. Asking the right questions and then listening with both head and heart got right to the core of the matter with most people. And it was *always* about so much more than money. Inevitably, meaning trumped money. *Life worth* always outweighed *net worth.*

Don't wait until you have your own "lost in the Serengeti" experience—divorce, death, job loss, a failed semester, or a sick child—in order to enlarge your perspective. Choose to take an accurate reading of your *life worth* now so you can make a balanced investment in each of your key life dimensions.

To do this, you have to practice a "salmon perspective"—swimming upstream against a rushing torrent of marketing and messaging to the contrary. But nothing wonderful is ever gained by taking it easy. It requires commitment on your part. Let me share something with you. It's worth it. Your life, thinking, and relationships will be transformed.

Jesus knew all about our natural inclination to fret about our finery and stew about our stuff—to live a one-coordinate life. That's why He cautioned His closest friends:

> Don't fuss about what's on the table at mealtimes
> or if the clothes in your closet are in fashion. There

is far more to your inner life than the food you put in your stomach, more to your outer appearance than the clothes you hang on your body. Look at the ravens, free and unfettered, not tied down to a job description, carefree in the care of God. *And you count far more.*[3]

Leading a *fully engaged* life begins with a multi-coordinate focus on your *life worth*—a realization that

Relationships matter more than anything.
Health determines your quality of life.
Work gives voice to your giftedness.
Hobbies engage your energy beyond work.
Learning animates your imagination.
And **Faith** gives all of your life purpose.

Nothing wonderful is ever gained by taking it easy. It requires commitment on your part.

To determine your current *life worth*, use the assessment that begins on the following page. There are 10 dimensions of *life worth*. Measure each one. Your life is worth so much more than money. Are you living like it?

DO *less*. BE *more*.

What Is Your *Life Worth*?

How satisfied are you with each life dimension listed below? How important are these life dimensions to you? Please rate each on a scale of 1–5 (1=low; 3=medium; 5=high).

	Satisfied	Important
HEALTH *Regular routines that promote healthy energy and vitality*	_____	_____
LEARNING *People and environments that stimulate growth*	_____	_____
FAMILY *Interest and involvement in the lives of family members*	_____	_____
WORK *Work that expresses talents and passion*	_____	_____
LOVE RELATIONSHIP *Alignment with loved one's values and dreams*	_____	_____
SPIRITUAL LIFE *Sense of purpose, relationship with God, and/or service to others*	_____	_____

	Satisfied	Important

FRIENDSHIPS
*Adequate number and depth
of relationships*

COMMUNITY
*Living in the place that matches
interests, relationships, and work*

VOLUNTEERING/HOBBIES
*Involvement that expresses interests
and/or desire to serve*

FINANCIAL
*Well-ordered finances that give
confidence and joy*

For scoring, go to page 165.

CHAPTER TWO

Share Your Story

Your life is a blog, not a book.

My friend Paul's dad celebrated his 100th birthday by playing 18 holes of golf with his three sons. His only concession to age was riding in a cart rather than carrying his clubs. Several weeks after his centennial golf outing, he renewed his local newspaper subscription for two years—the maximum allowable time. Death surprised him six months later. On the eve of his passing, he commented that he knew full well he would die someday, but he didn't think it would "happen so fast."

About a month before his father's death, Paul thought about his dad's story. Despite their close relationship, he realized that, for him, there were many gaps and incomplete chapters. So he sat down and constructed 37 interview questions in an effort to fill in his dad's life story.

Paul drove out to meet his dad, hoping to run through all his unanswered questions. After explaining his purpose, he popped the first question over lunch at a local restaurant.

George adjusted his hearing aid. Paul repeated the first question. There was a long pause, followed by a fractured response that communicated more discomfort than detail. Clearly his dad needed time for reflection in order to take on questions requiring the recall of facts and feelings about significant life events across a 100-year timeline.

So Paul decided to type the 37 questions and mail them

to his dad, gently encouraging him to take some quiet time to jot down answers in the ample white spaces.

Some of the things Paul wanted to know:

- What was your most pleasant childhood memory?
- Growing up, what did your family do for fun?
- Who was your best friend in high school— and what was he/she like?
- What did you two usually do together?
- Describe the time you first met Mom.
- What was it like to live on a ship at sea in wartime (WWII)?
- Did you lose any close friends during the war?
- What did you do during the first weeks after arriving at home?
- What was your greatest accomplishment during your 27 years as a high school principal?
- What is one thing you would do differently if you had the chance?
- When were you the happiest?
- The saddest?
- What advice do you have for those in retirement or approaching retirement?
- What advice would you give young parents today?

The list went on.

Paul planned to complete the interview when he returned from vacation. But that busy month ended with his dad's heart attack, short hospitalization, and unexpected passing.

Following the funeral, the family gathered in George's one-bedroom apartment, attempting to finalize his affairs and distribute items of sentimental value. Paul was cleaning out his desk when he came across the four-page document entitled "Some Questions for Dad."

His dad had completed the assignment, worthy of an A+. "My brothers and I got the answers we needed," Paul told me, "to fill the gaps and complete the chapters in Dad's life story. No question about it—the sight of that document, complete with his longhand responses, was the highlight of an afternoon filled with laughter and tears triggered by shared memories." What an amazing parting gift.

Suppose Paul had presented you with 37 life questions. Would you be able to share your own story?

- What's been your greatest moment?
- Biggest fear?
- How did you meet the love of your life?
- When have you been happiest?

- Saddest?
- What advice would you pass on to your children?
- Grandchildren?

Each of us has a great, unfinished life story. Your own narrative weaves together the story of *past* life-shaping events, vital *current* experiences, and inspiring dreams about the *future*.

Each of us has a great, unfinished life story. Your own narrative weaves together the story of *past* life-shaping events, vital *current* experiences, and inspiring dreams about the *future*. Living your life story—not that of your mother, father, partner, boss, friend, or siblings—empowers you to DO *less* and BE *more* to yourself and others.

Trouble is, many people cramp up when it comes to living or voicing their life story. Maybe you're one of them. Let me disable a few defenses so you can tell your story and get on with leading a *focused* life right here and right now.

"But it's just an ordinary story!"

In an unforgettable scene from the movie *Dead Poets Society,* Robin Williams' character uses the ploy of poetry to inspire a group of young men to begin to craft their own extraordinary life stories. He awakens their imagination with these words:

> We don't read and write poetry because it's cute. We read and write poetry because we are members of the human race. And the human race is filled with passion. Medicine, law, business, engineering—these are noble pursuits and necessary to sustain life. But poetry, beauty, romance, love—these are what we stay alive for.
>
> To quote from Whitman, "O me! O life! Of the questions of these recurring; of the endless trains of the faithless—of cities filled with the foolish; what good amid these, O me, O life? Answer. That you are here—that life exists, and identity; that the powerful play goes on and you may contribute a verse." That the powerful play goes on and you may contribute a verse. What will your verse be?

It's not about having a really great story or even about your whole story. It's about *your* story—*your* pivotal life events that impact your present but don't limit your future. If you want to be *fully engaged* yourself, it's vital to *know* your life story. If you want to engage others as a parent, leader, spouse, or friend, *share* your life story.

As remarkable as it may seem, your life story is not composed for your own entertainment. It was designed for the enjoyment and encouragement of others. The unique life experiences with which you're blessed are the perfect wisdom that will inspire someone else to act. But you need to contribute your one remarkable verse—TODAY!

The unique life experiences with which you're blessed are the perfect wisdom that will inspire someone else to act.

"I'll play it safe and stick to the facts!"

Facts are great, but they don't engage or transform you or anybody else. We are fogged in by *information*—overloaded with data, facts, and figures delivered by infinite search engine hits. What we really long for, however, is *wisdom*—knowledge revealed by narrative. With YouTube videos, instant messaging, blog posts, and Facebook walls, we've become our own news agencies.

But the information age in which we live deepens our craving for story. As writer Robert Dickman says, "A story is a fact wrapped in an emotion that can compel us to take action and so transform the world around us."[4]

Great stories are visual, emotional, and provoke an immediate and personal response. They draw you into the action. They quicken your pulse and animate your imagination. Stories are how you remember formative events, gain vital perspective, and pass on significant traditions. You cannot remain a passive spectator in your own story. No one else will. But you can't play it safe and merely give basic facts either. You need to wrap facts in emotion—the color commentary of your whole life.

I remember riding with my father two years ago and having him suddenly point to a house in what is now inner-city Milwaukee and state the fact, "That's where I grew up."

But then my dad continued to fill in the rest of the story. His father died suddenly when he was six years old. A year later, his mother lost their house and was forced to live in an upper flat and take in boarders to help pay the rent. My grandmother never did remarry, own another house, or get a driver's license. She worked hard all of her life to make ends meet. My father grew up fiercely independent and fatherless. Just these few details of my father's life story transformed my understanding of where he came from and how the circumstances of his life shaped him as a father, husband, coworker, and friend.

To withhold or dumb down your story is an act of pride or neglect. Oliver Wendell Holmes said, "Most people go to their graves with their music still inside them." To pass away without passing on your own story is like having the town library burn down—and its one-of-a-kind historical archives with it.

People in your life want to hear your life story. Share it! It will engage you and transform them.

Krista Tippett, host of the Peabody Award–winning radio show *On Being*, writes:

There are some truths that only mathematical equations can convey, and others that can be conveyed only by poetry. There is wisdom, too, that only story can capture. The most vivid personal stories have the most universal reach, elevating our sense of others and of the humanity we share.[5]

People in your life want to hear your life story. Share it! It will engage you and transform them.

"There are parts of my story I'd rather forget!"

When our son, Brett, was four years old, he was kicked out of the preschool carpool for spitting on another boy. Carol was horrified! As she gave me the blow-by-blow account of Brett's mischief, I patiently listened.

Then I calmly responded with, "Well, I did the same thing when I was in grade school. As a matter of fact, I was removed from the bus virtually every year until high school for similar spontaneously foolish acts."

As I recalled the incident, Carol's pointed response was an exasperated "I should have done a background check on you. Had I known all of your story, I might have made a different life choice!"

Fortunately, childhood mischief for both Brett and myself turned into adolescent meandering and eventually matured into a sense of adult mission. There is hope for all of us.

It's vital to know your past—your roots. Often those values and beliefs are sculpted in your early, formative years.

But your history doesn't determine your destiny. Historian David McCullough observes: "Nobody lived in the past, if you stop to think about it."[6] This is hugely important since many people attempt just the opposite—clinging tenaciously to past glories or refusing to release past failures. The fact is, we all live in the present.

Interestingly, the only question Paul's dad skipped was, "What is one thing you would do differently if you had the chance?" Paul envisions that his dad leapfrogged right over that one. It's not that he didn't make mistakes. He simply didn't have many regrets. He lived his life fully forward.

And so can you.

The good news is that your story is a blog, not a book. Chapters are added until you breathe your last. But, just like a blog, you must attend to adding regularly to your story or the content will go stale. The most closely followed blogs are active, breathing, inspiring, and provocative.

Use the following five questions to discover and articulate your Life Story. The result may be greater engagement and depth of communication with those people most important to you.

Your life is a blog, not a book. Are you writing your next chapter now?

DO *less*. BE *more*.

What's Your Life Story?

If you were to tell me the main events in your life story in just three minutes, what would you say?

Use the following five questions to discover and articulate your Life Story.

a—attitude

What is your attitude toward life? Is it positive or negative? A source of fun or fear? Where did your attitude toward life come from?

_____

_____

_____

e—experience

What were your earliest life experiences? Your most memorable experiences?

_____

_____

_____

i—important lessons

If you were facing your final days and you wanted to share with the next generation the three most important lessons you've learned about life, what would they be?

_____

_____

_____

o—outlook

Life is not a straight path from beginning to end, but rather a series of transitions, surprises, and challenges. What transitions are you expecting next in your life? (Examples: retirement, marriage, aging parents, children, graduation.) How are you preparing for these transitions?

_____

_____

_____

u—understanding

How well do you understand yourself, and the kind of life you'd like to pursue? Who have been your mentors?

_____

_____

_____

CHAPTER THREE

Do What Matters

Your values determine your choices.

US Airways Flight 1549 took off from LaGuardia Airport for Charlotte, North Carolina, at 3:26 p.m. on January 15, 2009. Less than a minute later, it flew through a flock of birds. With both engines out, Captain Chesley "Sully" Sullenberger and First Officer Jeff Skiles floated over New York City and pulled off the first successful emergency water landing of a commercial flight, gliding the crippled jetliner into the Hudson River. All 155 passengers were pulled to safety as the plane slowly sank into the waves.

"We had a miracle on 34th Street. I believe now we have had a miracle on the Hudson," Governor David Paterson said.[7]

Perhaps. Maybe it *was* a miracle. Divine intervention. A supernatural phenomenon.

Or maybe it was the payoff of Captain Sullenberger's values, sculpted by tragedy, that guided him to act as if 155 lives are worth far more than a $60 million US Airways jetliner. "Quite frankly," he said, "one of the reasons I think I've placed such a high value on life is that my father took his." Suffering from depression, Sully's father committed suicide in 1995.[8]

Captain Sullenberger's education began decades earlier. He graduated from the U.S. Air Force Academy and flew

F-4 fighter planes. Twelve of his fellow military pilots died on training exercises. While grieving their loss, Sully also went to school on their crashes.

The most common cause of pilot fatality was that they waited too long to eject. They would die before suffering the embarrassment or retribution of coming back empty-handed rather than with a multi-million-dollar jet. That sounds crazy, doesn't it? The pilots valued saving face more than their own life—right up until they lost it, auguring into the ground at Mach speed.

How often do we do the same thing, though—clinging tenaciously to work instead of balance, religion in place of real relationship, or routine in lieu of courageous action—right up until we run smack into reality? But clarifying our values can prevent the crash and inspire instead a *fully engaged* life.

What do I mean by *values*? The dictionary defines them as "deep longings and beliefs that a person acts on consistently." There are two critical and equally important parts to this description. Values represent what's important to you—"deep longings and beliefs." But, in order to truly be core values, there must also be an accompanying pattern of behavior—"consistent action."

Think of it this way. Have you ever seen any of the *CSI* TV shows? All of the shows follow an identical successful formula. In the first 60 seconds, something bad happens—someone falls out of a building, washes up on a beach, gets eaten by a shark. It's always tragic and, as the seasons drag on, increasingly outrageous. The remaining 59 minutes are devoted to determining if this was a crime, and if so, who perpetrated it.

How you spend your time and where you invest your money is indicative of your core values. Those values determine your choices. What does the evidence show? What really matters to you?

At exactly the 30-minute mark, a hapless suspect is confronted with a mountain of circumstantial evidence. He, of course, maintains his innocence. At this critical juncture, the CSI investigators always say, "Then you won't mind giving us a sample of your DNA!" In layperson's terms, DNA is our unique genetic fingerprint.

Your values are the DNA of your choices. The evidence to "convict" you of your values is revealed by the two most important currencies of your life—your time and money.

The proof is in your calendar and record of financial activity. How you spend your time and where you invest your money is indicative of your core values. Those values determine your choices. What does the evidence show? What really matters to you?

When we are unfocused, we lack passion and conviction. We allow our circumstances, the demands of work, or even loved ones to dictate our choices. We don't take a stand because we are unclear about what really matters, or, more likely, we lack the moral courage to stand up and take the heat for an unpopular or potentially even dangerous choice.

Standing firm on values almost always requires moral courage and eventual sacrifice. As Bill George, former CEO and chairman of Medtronic, Inc., said,

> The values that form the basis for authentic leadership are derived from your beliefs and convictions, but you will not know what your true values are until they are tested under pressure. When your success, your career, or even your life hangs in the balance, you learn what is most important, what you are prepared to sacrifice, and what trade-offs you are willing to make.[9]

Values are at the heart of leading a *fully engaged* life. Focus comes down to a matter of integrity—of being a whole person. The dictionary defines integrity as "the quality or state of being complete or undivided." This is critical. When you are living with integrity, your life is energy-giving, rather than energy-sapping, because your efforts flow directly from your core values.

If you lack integrity, you aren't firing on all cylinders in your work, relationships, spiritual life, or health. Your confidence with self and engagement with others are sure to be lacking. You're less than a whole person.

|in·te·gri·ty|
The quality or state of being complete or undivided.

Jesus spoke regularly about living in alignment with our values. On integrity with money, He said:

> "If you're honest in small things,
>   you'll be honest in big things;
> If you're a crook in small things,
>   you'll be a crook in big things.

If you're not honest in small jobs,
    who will put you in charge of the store?
No worker can serve two bosses:
    He'll either hate the first and love the second
Or adore the first and despise the second.
You can't serve both God and the Bank."

When the Pharisees, a money-obsessed bunch, heard him say these things, they rolled their eyes, dismissing him as hopelessly out of touch.[10]

Far from being out of touch, Jesus was speaking truth to power regarding the life currency that we most often abuse. While time is our most precious resource—you can never make more time—money is the currency that causes us most often to go against our values and abuse time.

Clarity of values allows you to DO *less* and BE *more*. It empowers you to say "yes" to what matters, "no" to what is unimportant, and then to stick with your yes and no.

But these choices often cause a good deal of stress.

Best-selling author John Ortberg describes the tension this way:

We live in the tension between our desire to have the good life and our desire to be a good person.

A fascinating place to see this tension on display is to open up a newspaper and compare ads with obituaries. Ads tell us: "here's how to have great hair, great teeth, great clothes, great food, great sex, great cars and great bodies." But obituaries never say: "he had great hair, great teeth, great clothes, great food, great sex, great cars and a great body." We want to be good people, but we're willing to give it up to have the good life. We want to *have* what is offered in the ads, but *be* what is spoken in the obituaries.[11]

Clarity of values and courage of conviction help us to alleviate this tension.

But here's where it gets tricky. We don't simply wake up one day and decide, "Yep. This is *the* day. I'm going to get crystal clear on my values as of (fill in today's date)!"

Clarity of values empowers you to say "yes" to what matters, "no" to what is unimportant, and then to stick with your yes and no.

Values are almost always formed early in life. We catch our core values from parents, grandparents, mentors, and models. Most of our life values are in place by the time we reach adolescence. But if you ask most people what their values are, you get a "deer in the headlights look" from them.

"Our values are so much an intrinsic part of our lives and behavior," say William Guth and Renato Tagiuri, "that we are often unaware of them—or, at least, we are unable to think about them clearly and articulately. Yet our values, along with other factors, clearly determine our choices."[12]

Values often come into sharp focus in times of stress. Difficult times don't just display our values; they distill them to their very essence. So if you want to be really clear on what matters, just introduce some serious stress and then watch what happens!

As an alternative to introducing real stress, use the Life Values sort on the next page to discover your core values. The result, if consistently lived out, will be a life of greater engagement and fulfillment.

Your values determine your choices. What are you choosing today?

DO *less*. BE *more*.

What Are Your Life Values?

Your values serve as a vital foundation for living a truly focused life. Follow the two steps outlined in this inventory to discover where your values come from, what they are, and to identify values that, if practiced more consistently, would give you greater fulfillment.

Step One: Where did your values come from?

Identify three people who have had the deepest impact on your life (at least one outside your family). What specific advice, philosophy, or value has stuck with you?

Name_____

Value_____

Name_____

Value_____

Name_____

Value_____

List three books, tapes, movies, poems, sermons, or sayings that have contributed to your own values. What insight has stayed with you?

Resource _____

Insight _____

Resource _____

Insight _____

Resource _____

Insight _____

List three experiences that have profoundly shaped your life direction. What value did each experience teach you?

Experience _____

Value _____

Experience _____

Value _____

Experience _____

Value _____

Step Two: What are your values?

With your experiences and important people in mind, check 10 Life Values from the following list that resonate most with you and reflect how you actually live your life. Or, add your own values in the Other areas. Next, circle the five Life Values you feel are most important for you to consistently practice.

LIFE VALUES

Achievement	Accuracy
Adventure	Aesthetics
Balance	Beauty
Change	Contribution
Connectedness	Comradeship
Entrepreneuring	Empowerment
Elegance	Faith
Free Time	Freedom
Imaginativeness	Inclusivity
Intellectual Status	Health
Humor	Honesty
Leadership	Leisure
Mentoring	Nurturing
Participation	Performance
Productivity	Power
Responsibility	Renewal
Self-Expression	Spirituality
Stability	Teaming
Trust	Vitality
Other:	Other:

Acknowledgment	Advancement
Authenticity	Autonomy
Caring	Challenge
Collaboration	Community
Creativity	Directness
Excellence	Excitement
Family Happiness	Focus
Friendship	Growth
Integrity	Independence
Helping Others	Helping Society
Joy	Knowledge
Location	Loyalty
Orderliness	Partnership
Peace	Playfulness
Precision	Recognition
Risk Taking	Security
Service	Success
Time Freedom	Tradition
Wealth	Wisdom
Other:	Other:

ALIGNMENT

*How does what you have
and what you do match what
you really want out of life?*

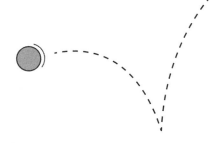

CHAPTER FOUR

Occupy Your Space

Your work is a calling.

The bumper sticker reads, *I owe, I owe, so it's off to work I go.* Millions of unemployed Americans would be happy to work, even to just pay off debt. And yet, to be *fully engaged* requires more than mere employment. It demands a dogged pursuit of calling.

A job, as defined by the dictionary, is "a paid position of regular employment." Many people work for money. Work provides the economic engine for a larger life. My friend and business partner, Richard Leider, wrote 10 years ago that he was "struck by the number of people who work hard to make fast money to gain the freedom *not* to work."[13] Their mantra seems to be "when I *have* enough, I'll *do* what I really want to do and I'll *be* happy."

Except that "having enough" never is. This is a doom loop—one that will never end and never satisfy. Few people, especially in the current economic climate, are making fast money if they are blessed to be working at all.

Did you know that the active verb for the word *job* is *jobbed*, which means "to be betrayed"? That's because so many people trade chasing a pension for pursuing their passion that they end up feeling jobbed when the work goes away, goes off shore, or continues endlessly with little enjoyment.

The word *career* comes from the French word *carrier,* meaning "race course," and the Latin word *carrus,* meaning "wheeled vehicle." For many, a career has evolved to just that—a never-ending series of left turns at ever-increasing speeds around a closed loop. "If you're just chasing the rabbit around the course, you're not running toward anything meaningful."[14]

"Having enough" never is.

A career can become a doom loop as well. The only difference is that the loop is longer and the speed is quicker.

NBC *Nightly News* closes each week with an inspiring feature titled, "Making a Difference." During the heartbreaking cascade of tragic news following the earthquake in Haiti, one "Making a Difference" featured Dr. Basil Jackson, a 78-year-old pediatric psychologist from Milwaukee, Wisconsin. Working in the most difficult circumstances imaginable, Dr. Jackson used his gift of healing and passion to touch countless poor children at the Port-au-Prince Medical Trauma Center. This was neither a job nor a career. It was a high calling.

Dr. Jackson described himself as an old man with a deep faith. But he added, "Faith doesn't count unless you do something about it in your behavior and your actions." He was *fully engaged*—thriving in the direst circumstances.

John Ortberg describes this sort of thriving as "the joy I know when my level of challenges reaches the level of my gifts, and I am consumed by neither boredom nor anxiety, but simply grace."[15] To hear your calling, and more importantly, to respond in courageous, obedient action to that calling, is to truly live in grace.

Best-selling author Po Bronson spent two years interviewing 900 people with the simple but provocative question, "What should I do with my life?" These were people of all classes, ages, and professions. The interviews were conducted immediately following the last recession in the U.S. The responses of 70 interviewees were published in his book by the same title.

One startling conclusion Bronson reached was this:

> I'm convinced that business success in the future starts with the question "What should I do with my life?" People thrive by focusing on the question of who they really are—and connecting that to work that they truly love (and, in so doing, unleashing a productive and creative power that they never imagined).[16]

How would you answer Po's provocative question? Are you confident that you are doing what you should do with your life? Your answer will have a significant impact on your personal engagement and ultimately on your sense of fulfillment.

In marketing terms, a brand that is enduring and robust, especially in a down economy, is said to "fully occupy its space." Do you fully occupy your space in your work? Is your brand enduring, even distinct, in this down market? The key to achieving maximum occupancy is to be engaged in the right work—the occupation that is your *calling*. To work with a sense of *calling* is to answer the question "What should I do with my life?" with a resounding, "Exactly what I'm doing right now!" And it is doing just that—and no more. Called people are seldom overcommitted.

In her classic novel, *Out of Africa,* Isak Dinesen gives a moving description of feeling called:

> Up in this high air you breathed easily, drawing in a vital assurance and lightness of heart. In the highlands you woke up in the morning and thought: *Here I am, where I ought to be.*[17]

Calling is the powerful intersection of passion and motivated abilities. Your passion elicits powerful emotions and authentically focuses your deepest attention—to the extent that you can lose track of time ("It's already lunchtime! You've got to be kidding!").

Passionate work is work you love to do—work you are motivated to do. It enhances your feeling of value to others and increases your satisfaction.

Called people are seldom overcommitted.

Activities others compliment you on are often fueled by your strengths. Motivated abilities are who you truly are. When you work in the sweet spot of passion and motivated abilities, you tend to deliver great service and uncommon value.

To build and focus your work in the heart of your *calling* is to fully *occupy your space*.

I love this timeless prescription from the apostle Paul for discovering your *calling*:

> Make a careful exploration of who you are and the work you have been given, and then sink yourself into that. Don't be impressed with yourself. Don't compare yourself with others. Each of you must take responsibility for doing the creative best you can with your own life.[18]

Let's break down his suggested path to fully occupying your space together.

Make a careful exploration of who you are.

Each one of us has strengths—the unique pattern of natural gifts, talents, and skills acquired through education, life, and work experiences. *Calling* begins with knowing who you are and how you're wired to contribute.

...and the work you've been given.

We also each have a unique vocation, a place where we can give powerful voice to our strengths. Where is that place? Frederick Buechner defines *calling* as: "The place God calls you to is the place where your deep gladness and the world's deep hunger meet."[19]

Sink yourself into it.

Fully occupy your space! Focus intently on your gifts.

Don't be too impressed with yourself.

A good friend cautioned me after I had given perhaps the most important speech of my career, "Guard your heart today. Don't let pride in. Remember the gap between how good you really are at this and how great it went!" Great advice! The day immediately after a significant high is the most dangerous day. We can be easily fooled into believing it is all about us.

Don't compare yourself with others.

Calling is an inside job. Called people work from a place of integrity within themselves, from their hearts. Jazz saxophone great Charlie Parker said, "If it ain't in your heart, it ain't in your horn." It's not about comparing yourself to others. It's about knowing and then voicing your own motivated strengths. Put what's in your heart in your horn. Forget about what others say!

Each of you must take responsibility for doing the creative best you can with your own life.

Saint Francis de Sales wrote, "God requires a faithful fulfillment of the merest trifle given us to do rather than the most ardent aspiration to things to which we are not called."[20]

Each of us has a *calling*. Most of us don't get an epiphany or have it delivered to us by a cosmic skywriter. We get a faint whisper, an urge, a tug. Strengths provide direction and passion gives us the fuel to persevere.

But when that urge comes, you need to act boldly and strike out in the direction of the call.

DO *less* of all the periphery tasks or jobs in order to BE *more* of who you are uniquely called to be.

> **It's not about comparing yourself to others. It's about knowing and then voicing your own motivated strengths.**

Use the following *Calling Cards*® exercise as a simple but elegant way to determine the intersection of your passion and giftedness. The results may show you how to strengthen your work and effectively manage your time and energy in order to enjoy greater engagement with fulfillment.

Your work is a *calling*. Are you passionately voicing your gifts?

DO *less*. BE *more*.

Calling Cards®

Using the *Calling Cards*® helps you to name your *calling*—the intersection of passion and giftedness—and, as a result, to work with greater focus and enjoyment. The cards are organized in six environments, called Holland's Code. Use the following three steps to determine your *calling*.

List of Calling Cards

Artistic

Performing Events

Creating Things

Writing Things

Seeing the Big Picture

Composing Themes

Seeing Possibilities

Designing Things

Breaking Molds

Adding Humor

Realistic

Moving Physically

Solving Problems

Growing Things

Shaping Environments

Making Things Work

Fixing Things

Building Things

Enterprising

Making Deals

Starting Things

Empowering Others

Managing Things

Selling Intangibles

Bringing Out Potential

Opening Doors

Exploring the Way

Persuading People

Conventional

Straightening Things Up

Doing the Numbers

Processing Things

Operating Things

Getting Things Right

Organizing Things

Social

Healing Wounds

Getting Participation

Resolving Disputes

Instructing People

Giving Care

Building Relationships

Helping Overcome Obstacles

Creating Dialogue

Creating Trust

Bringing Joy

Awakening Spirit

Facilitating Change

Investigative

Analyzing Information

Translating Things

Putting the Pieces Together

Making Connections

Investigating Things

Getting to the Heart of Matters

Researching Things

Discovering Resources

Advancing Ideas

STEP ONE

Go through the lists and answer this question: *Is this something I am truly passionate about?* Cross out any callings that do not motivate and inspire you.

STEP TWO

Focusing only on the callings that are not crossed out, answer this second question: *Is this something in which I am truly gifted?* Circle those responses that reflect your natural gifts.

STEP THREE

From among the circled responses only, choose the five callings you feel strongest about and write them in descending order, with the top item being the best description of your calling—work that best describes your gifts and passion.

- _____
- _____
- _____
- _____
- _____

***Calling* Practices:** Answer these questions: *What is my top Calling Card? How can I focus my time and work to make the best use of my calling? With whom do I need to partner in order to focus more energy on my calling?*

To learn more or to order decks of *Calling Cards*® from The Inventure Group, go to **www.inventuregroup.com** and visit the store.

CHAPTER FIVE

Dream Wide Awake

Your dreams inspire movement.

Like most 15-year-olds, John Goddard had no shortage of dreams. What set him apart was that one rainy afternoon he sat down at his kitchen table and wrote them down—127 dreams in all—and then proceeded over the next generation to accomplish 109 of his original quests.

Goddard's list was no garden-variety fare. He envisioned climbing the world's highest peaks, exploring from source to mouth the longest rivers of the world, trekking on every continent, flying a variety of aircraft, tracing his family roots, and even lighting a match with a .22 rifle!

"When I was 15," he told a *Life* magazine reporter, "all the adults I knew seemed to complain, 'Oh, if I'd only done this or that when I was younger.' They had let life slip by them. I was sure that if I planned for it, I could have a life of excitement and fun and knowledge."[21] Goddard's desire was to live a life of no regrets.

Dreams ignite our spirit of aliveness. They are vital to our physical, mental, and spiritual health. Without dreams, we lose our connection to the past and our hope for the future. Dreams are the fuel for leading a *focused* life. When aligned with values, dreams can re-ignite passion and provide the necessary inspiration to thrive at any life stage and in any circumstance.

Brett, our older son, was tasked his sophomore year in high school with creating a 50:50 list—50 things he wanted to do before age 50. As you might imagine, the 16-year-old mind can dream up some incredible ideas. But over time this has become less of an adolescent fantasy and more of a blueprint for his life—rich in ideas for passionate pursuits.

When aligned with values, dreams can re-ignite passion and provide the necessary inspiration to thrive at any life stage and in any circumstance.

Now, at age 27, Brett has accomplished 20 of his original 50 dreams, moved several items off his list as unattainable or no longer interesting, added new quests, and used his list as a serious bargaining chip in negotiating for bold new life adventures. The latest item to be checked off this past summer was #13—"Marry the girl of my dreams."

He is dreaming wide awake!

You may be thinking, *Isn't constructing a Life Dream list seriously out of sync with the title of this book— DO less, BE more?*

If this looks suspiciously like a prescription to DO *more*—or at least to feel the self-imposed burden of attempting a moonshot of experiences, instead of focusing intently on what really matches your passion, giftedness, and sense of calling in this world—bear with me for a moment.

You can read about the greatest setup for the ultimate 50:50 list in the encounter between the newly appointed King of Israel and God. He approaches Solomon in a dream with the open-ended request, "Ask for *whatever* you want me to give you."[22] In other words, "dream big. The holy checkbook is open, and the celestial calendar is cleared. So, Solomon, what's on your list? No request is too big." What would your response be?

What was Solomon's answer? "Give me a *God-listening heart* so I can lead your people well, discerning the difference between good and evil."[23]

Whoa! No epic adventure to New Zealand? No breakfast with Nelson Mandela? No front-row seats at Eric Clapton rocking Royal Albert Hall? Not even a winning lottery ticket?

Nope. "Just" wisdom. As a result, God grants Solomon wisdom—but also wealth, glory, and a long life.

Here's the radical departure from most motivational rah-rah encouragements to dream big: Let passion and a sense of purpose be the focal point of your dreams, not just a selfish pursuit. John Ortberg suggests we "pursue a dream borne out of a burden."[24]

Blake Mycoskie already had the gift of being a serial entreperneur. At age 19 he had started a door-to-door laundry service while still a student at Southern Methodist University. He followed this by establishing an advertising agency, a reality TV show, and a very successful on-line drivers' education school for teens. It would seem that he was checking one item after another off of his 50:50 list.

But then, when he was age 29, the sight of sores on barefoot children in Argentina created a new vision. Blake launched TOMS Shoes, whose name evolved from the company's original slogan, "Shoes for tomorrow," as a response to the burden in his heart and the glaring social need he saw. The trip to Argentina was the catalyst for the natural intersection of his entrepreneurial giftedness and passion to make a difference in the world.

As of September 2010, TOMS Shoes has given one million pairs of new shoes to children in 25 countries through its "One for One" movement—for every pair of shoes TOMS sells, the company gives a pair away to a needy child. Blake's dream, borne out of a burden, is a blessing to countless children worldwide.

"What you can plan is too small for you to live."

—DAVID WHYTE, *Crossing the Unknown Sea*

Eugene and Minhee Cho and their three young children are an "average, middle-class" family in Seattle. They grew up knowing all of the statistics about the rich-poor disparity in the world:

- Approximately 2.7 billion people live on less than $2 U.S. per day.
- Approximately 9.2 million children (25,000 each day) under the age of 5 die each year, mostly from preventable diseases.
- 2.5 billion people do not have access to adequate sanitation, and about 900 million do not have access to clean water.
- 75 million people do not have access to education.
- Nearly 11,500 people die every day from HIV/AIDS, tuberculosis, and malaria.

But it was traveling to impoverished places in Burma, Southeast Asia, Africa, and Central America and seeing it with their own eyes that transformed the Cho family. It wasn't merely the overwhelming extreme poverty that touched them, but also the hope and courage of people working to lift themselves out of such circumstances.

It was these realities and the amazing stories of courage and hope that compelled the Chos to make a life decision in 2009—to start One Day's Wages.[25] They donated their 2009 income ($68,000) to the cause of fighting extreme global poverty as a public declaration that they were putting their money where their dream is.

And that dream? To encourage family, friends, and the rest of the world to donate one day's wages, approximately 0.4% of their annual income, to fight the ravages of extreme global poverty.

How about you? What are your dreams? Sometimes our capacity to dream is diminished by life's circumstances. Life is an improvisational art. We have to make it up as we go. If we are not dreaming big, we risk dying small. Your dreams are the inspiration for movement. "Yet somewhere along the way, most of us stop living out of imagination and start living out of memory. We stop creating the future and start repeating the past."[26]

**Life is an improvisational art.
We have to make it up as we go.
If we are not dreaming big, we risk
dying small.**

Helen Keller observed that "the most pathetic person in the world is someone who has sight but has no vision." Too often, we get caught up in the tyranny of the urgent or the illusion of the impossible. As a result, we confine our dreams to the night and then sleepwalk through the day. We are not only sleep-starved but also dream-deprived.

How do you acquire a fresh set of eyes to see and a new heart to feel the burden of a noble dream? I fly over 100,000 miles per year for business. For many years, my travel preference was an aisle seat for more legroom and a quicker escape at the flight's end. I would seldom gaze out the window because I thought I'd seen it all before. Denver looks like Minneapolis, which resembles San Francisco and New York. It's all the same from 30,000 feet.

Then, one day recently, I sat across from a little girl and her mother on a short evening flight to Chicago. I couldn't help but hear her awe-filled exclamations of "Mommy, look at *THAT*!" as we descended out of the gray mist and flat light to the twinkling lights below.

Having a fresh set of eyes, undimmed by the passage of time and the pace of life events, is crucial to seeing the burdens of the world that only our dreams can address. I have since changed my seating preference back to window and worry a lot less about being first off the plane after landing.

Uncertain times can cause constricted thinking and overly cautious living. In spite of the times we live in, we must dream wide awake. And our dreams must be anchored in a burden we see and feel.

Use the following exercise as a model for casting your Life Dreams. You have nothing to lose and everything to gain—a reinvigorated, refocused life.

Your dreams inspire movement. What's stirring in your heart today?

DO *less*. BE *more*.

What Are Your Life Dreams?

Use the following examples to seed your imagination.

Health

- ☐ Eat family dinners at home.
- ☐ Run a marathon for a cause.
- ☐ Hire a fitness coach.
- ☐ _____
- ☐ _____

Friendships

- ☐ Go on an annual friends' adventure.
- ☐ Take a friend to coffee each week.
- ☐ Reconnect with high school buddies.
- ☐ _____
- ☐ _____

Family

- ☐ Travel with parents.
- ☐ Plan a family reunion.
- ☐ Reconcile with siblings.
- ☐ _____
- ☐ _____

Volunteering/Hobbies

- ☐ Adopt a stray.
- ☐ Volunteer as a mentor.
- ☐ Take a short-term mission trip.
- ☐ _____
- ☐ _____

Love Relationship

- ☐ Go on date nights.
- ☐ Plan my 50th wedding anniversary.
- ☐ Embrace my wife's favorite hobby.
- ☐ _____
- ☐ _____

Spiritual Life

- ☐ Read the Bible cover-to-cover.
- ☐ Find a spiritual director.
- ☐ Meditate daily.
- ☐ _____
- ☐ _____

Learning

- ☐ Read 3 daily newspapers.
- ☐ Learn a second language.
- ☐ Journal regularly.
- ☐ _____
- ☐ _____

Community

- ☐ Coach a youth sports team.
- ☐ Help clean up the neighborhood.
- ☐ Plant a vegetable garden.
- ☐ _____
- ☐ _____

Work

- ☐ Work abroad.
- ☐ Find a mentor.
- ☐ Discover my calling.
- ☐ _____
- ☐ _____

Financial

- ☐ Get a realistic retirement plan.
- ☐ Finance a clinic in Haiti.
- ☐ Organize my financial/estate documents.
- ☐ _____
- ☐ _____

CHAPTER SIX

Drop the Ball

Your life is more than just showing up.

everal years ago, I was facilitating a leadership program for a group of American executives in Shanghai. By the third day, the whole class was feeling the full effects of jet lag, so I decided to try an experiment to jump-start our flagging energy and sleeping brain synapses early the next morning.

We were staying in a hotel directly across from People's Park—a beautiful urban setting in central Shanghai filled with monuments, gardens, walkways, and ponds. Every dawn, the park springs to life with people strolling, doing tai chi, flying kites, playing table tennis, engaging in conversation, fishing, and simply hanging out. My harebrained idea was to have all of the leaders take a silent 30- to 45-minute walk through the park, observing people and their surroundings at daybreak, and then report back with what they saw, heard, and felt.

The operative word here is *observe.* Almost every leader emerged from the elevator doing the "BlackBerry® prayer" as they prepared to take a silent walk intended to heighten their observation and awareness. I stood at the door with a shopping bag to collect their omnipresent technological weaponry before they set out to walk through People's Park. I was met with looks of horror, anger, and plain confusion! "You mean you want me to walk silently *without* my Black-

Berry®? For *30 minutes*? Are you *crazy*? What if the office *needs* me?"

It was a humorous but sad reality. Like many people today, these leaders couldn't envision being disconnected, even for 30 minutes, from the tentacles of their technology.

The late American novelist, David Foster Wallace, tells the story of two young fish swimming along when an older, wiser fish passes them and inquires, "How's the water?" The two young fish continue on until one eventually turns to the other and asks, "What the heck is water?"[27]

We are so busy, distracted, overwhelmed, and emotionally absent that we don't even recognize the water in which we are swimming. We just believe the lie that "This is the way it is—or has to be—to keep up." We believe that busier is better...or certainly necessary. The water we are swimming in is teeming with bad assumptions:

- *safety* (busy kids are safe kids)
- *advancement* (busy lives look better on job and college applications)
- *appearance* (I'm important because I'm busy and always connected to the office)
- *approval* (to be less frenetic would risk the disdain of my busier coworkers and friends)

All of this commotion and connectivity is resulting in sleep-deprived, busy-addicted, technology-tethered, relationship-starved people.

The single most mind-altering tool is the Internet, as it delivers precisely the kind of sensory and cognitive stimuli—repetitive, intensive, interactive, addictive—that have been shown to result in strong and rapid alterations in brain circuits and functions.[28]

The World Wide Web is literally rewiring our brains.

Did You Know...? **The average person checks his or her e-mail 37 times per day. The most recognized sound in the world is the ding of e-mail landing in your inbox, triggering the Pavlovian urge to immediately respond.**

A friend and client recently suggested that "technology is the new idolatry" after seeing a fellow churchgoer walking up to communion while covertly working his Black-Berry. And how's worshipping this new god working out for people?

> A study done in the UK in 2005 found that workers distracted by e-mail and voice mail suffered a fall in IQ more than twice that found in regular marijuana smokers.[29]

> The benefits of multitasking are more myth than fact.

- "What now passes for multitasking was once just called 'not paying attention.'"[30]
- The University of Utah found that drivers speaking on mobile phones are as impaired as drunk drivers.
- "It takes an average of 23 minutes and 15 seconds to get back on task" after having your work interrupted by something unrelated.[31]

As with every religion, there is a whole lexicon to describe the humorous but unhealthy demands of this god: "Deskfast, cup-holder cuisine, hurry sickness, presenteeism." There is even a prescribed worship posture: the "BlackBerry® prayer."

The danger of following this false god extends well beyond being dumber, distracted, or driving like you're drunk.

In business, excessive busyness is corrosive to reflection, which, in turn, inhibits creativity, the wellspring of breakthrough ideas and sustainable leadership.

Family life also falls prey to being overscheduled and undernourished:

> Time together is food for the family and we are in a state of "time famine" in daily life these days. What's strange about this, culturally, is that it has become a boast: "Oh, you think your family's busy! You should see mine!"[32]

Being fully present is increasingly unusual, and truly a gift to yourself and to the person you are honoring with your full attention.

Even the current state of marriage (49 percent of marriages end in divorce), health (two-thirds of Americans are obese or overweight), and education (1.2 million students fail to graduate from high school each year) trace part of the root cause of failure to being too busy to talk, exercise, eat healthy, or show up for class.

Richard Foster observes:

> We pant through an endless series of appointments and duties. The problem is especially acute for those who sincerely want to do what is right. With frantic fidelity, we respond to all calls to service, distressingly unable to distinguish the call of Christ from that of human manipulators. We feel bowed low with the burden of integrity.[33]

A pivotal guiding principle of leading *focused* lives is pace—moving at the proper speed. Clearly nothing happens if we do not show up at all. But showing up at the right moments, the teachable moments, requires moving at the right speed. How do we find the right rhythm? How do we show up at the impactful moments in the lives of our family, partners, associates, and friends?

Proper pace precedes authentic presence.

I had a meeting with one of my favorite business leaders a few years ago. Picture this scene—he had a corner office with a sofa, chair, and table. Beautiful artwork adorned three walls, and a large window framing downtown Atlanta occupied the fourth. There was no phone, clock, desk, or file cabinet.

For our one-hour meeting, he was fully present. No distractions. No interruptions. No cell phone buzzing or e-mail beeping. We accomplished more in 60 minutes than I get done with some people in a year. I left his office thinking, *How rare was that? What a gift!* Being fully present is increasingly unusual, and truly a gift to yourself and to the person you are honoring with your full attention.

What about you? How often are you fully present? You can appear at home but still be present in the office. You can show up for morning meditation but still be spiritually asleep. You can physically show up anywhere but still be light-years away emotionally or intellectually.

Leading a *focused* life requires authentic presence. We can't "fake it until we make it." Superficiality will not do:

> Superficiality is the curse of our age. The doctrine of instant satisfaction is a primary spiritual problem. The desperate need today is not for a greater number of intelligent people, or gifted people, but for *deep* people.[34]

And this depth of spirit begins with operating at a healthy pace and giving others our full presence.

This, of course, is all way easier said than done. The gravitational pull of busyness is strong. My suggestion? Drop the ball! Stop trying to master all the various dimensions of your life at all times. Giving equal and top priority to relationships, work, health, family, and yourself simultaneously is a prescription for disaster.

We need to DO *less,* WAY *less,* in order to BE *more* to ourselves and to the other important people in our life.

On the following page are a few tips I've observed in others that will help you determine which balls to drop in order to keep your most cherished ones in the air. The result may be that you do a consistently good job of managing your pace and presence as opposed to being in a continual state of siege by your calendar and e-mail.

Your life is more than just showing up. Are you fully present today?

DO *less.* BE *more.*

The 3 Ps

Pace

Our younger son, Josh, spent a year in South Africa, working with children in an orphanage and pitching in wherever and however he could. In a recent blog post titled "Learning to Walk with Others," he shared his initial doubts about the importance of his time there. He didn't feel he was having any measurable impact.

But then, after slowing down and simply "walking" with his brothers and sisters in their small South African village, he observed:

> I have to admit I was a little taken aback that my very being present was so impactful to those around me. Despite having no physical proof that I have accomplished anything, I suddenly felt like I had accomplished a great deal.
>
> I finally understand what "accompaniment" means. It is not about getting things done, fixing walls, teaching English, coaching soccer, or anything in the physical sense. It is about walking together with others. It is about entering into an unknown

path where we don't know where the road will lead, but we will walk it together.

I did not come here to start anything big and grand. God is already here, and by His grace He has asked me to join in what He is already doing.

The key is to WALK, not run. Try slowing down your pace a little for a day. See what happens in your own energy and relationships with others.

Presence

No matter what your religion or cultural background, set aside one day of rest each week. The story is that after creating the world in six days, God rested on the seventh. If it worked for Him, maybe it will for you too! After all, are you in the world-creating business?

Set aside one day each week where you turn off the technology and do no work—where you hang out with family and friends and check *nothing* off your list. The goal is to be *fully present* with the most important people in your life for a whole day. Force yourself, if you must, to enjoy each other's company and the world around you.

A great way to grow into a Sabbath day is to practice full presence in meetings, phone conversations, and any other interactions with others. Turn off the call waiting and tune out the technology. Watch how much more you accomplish and feel the joy of intimate connections with others.

Promise

Integrity is keeping the *small* promises you make to yourself and others. We undermine our full engagement by making too many promises and then breaking far too many of them. A *fully engaged* person is seldom overcommitted.

Over 20 years ago, I heard a conference speaker refer to the lifesaving word *NO!* Living a *focused* life requires you to get accomplished at saying and sticking with "NO" to peripheral things so you can commit to "YES" with the right things.

Look back at the *Life Worth* assessment you completed at the end of chapter 1. Which life dimensions are most important to you? Begin saying "YES" to activities and commitments that grow and nurture these dimensions and "NO" to ones that distract and diminish less important dimensions. Drop some balls in order to keep airborne what matters most to your loved ones and you.

ACTION

*How do you move
toward an exhilarating future?*

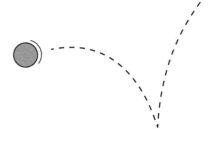

CHAPTER SEVEN

Celebrate Your Setbacks

Your engagement is fueled by failure.

For 13 years, Steve was really lost. He wandered homeless, panhandled on street corners, and mugged strangers for money to buy his next crack fix. His drug and alcohol use accelerated from recreational to habitual after his older brother slammed into a parked dump truck at 50 mph, shearing off the car's roof. When his younger brother committed suicide, Steve descended into the cycle of treatment, halfway houses, and relapse. Every attempt to arrest his free fall back into drugs was met with self-inflicted failure. After more than a dozen treatment centers and countless homeless shelters, he had burned up the system, had nothing left to sell, and no one left to call.

When Steve wandered shoeless into the Salvation Army, he was greeted at the door with "Welcome. We're so glad you're here!" That evening at chapel, one man put his arm around Steve, gazed directly into his eyes, and said, "I'm here to tell you that your nightmare is over."

Desperately needing that to be true but not believing it possible, Steve replied, "Look, buddy, this isn't my first rodeo. I've been in and out of treatment for years."

The man repeated, "You're not listening! I'm here to tell you that your nightmare is over. The horror story you've been living is over."

At that moment, the seeds of a *focused* life were planted.

Seven years later, Steve is clean and sober, joyfully married, and reinvesting daily right back where he was saved—at the Minneapolis Salvation Army—because "the ground there is so fertile for transformation." Steve was dead. Now he is alive—fully alive. When he recounts his journey, his eyes dance with the joy of being *truly focused* in his life, work, relationships, and faith.

Few stories of life transformation are as dramatic. Few people are as desperate as Steve was. But each of us longs for something more—something different. We have a deep desire to live a life of significance and meaning—a life where we're *focused* and satisfied.

We have a deep desire to live a life of significance and meaning—a life where we're *focused* and satisfied.

I'm not recommending 13 years of crack-addicted hell as the preferred route to fulfillment! But the paradox is that it often takes hardships, setbacks, or tragedy to ignite in us the resilience to relentlessly pursue a *focused* life. We can sleepwalk through days, even weeks, and not know the full extent of our disengagement. It's like the Northwest Airlines pilots that flew past Minneapolis by 150 miles on their way from San Diego before they realized they were over Wisconsin. The autopilot had lulled them to sleep.

What is your relationship with difficulty, setback, or failure? When you are honest with yourself, is there any influence in your life more powerful at forging your beliefs and inspiring your full engagement than failure?

In Pat Conroy's book about his dismal basketball season at the Citadel that saw only eight victories in 25 games, he observes:

> Loss is a fiercer, more uncompromising teacher, coldhearted but clear-eyed in its understanding that life is more dilemma than game and more trial than free pass. My acquaintance with loss has sustained me during the stormy passages of my life when the pink slips came through the door, when the checks bounced at the bank, when I told my small children I was leaving their mother, when the despair caught up with me, when the dreams of suicide began feeling like love songs of release. Though I learned some things from the games we won that year, I learned much, much more from loss.[35]

The crucible of loss forges the crucial resilience that will fuel a consistently *focused* life. Adversity introduces us to ourselves.

I was recently on a bus shuttling a group of leaders to an offsite workshop. The person sitting next to me, in an attempt to make conversation, said, "So, *you're* the leadership consultant." (I love that opening line—usually delivered with a hint of sarcasm!) Then he asked, "What do you think is the most important characteristic a leader must possess to be successful?"

My honest response was, "She or he must have been broken—physically, spiritually, professionally, personally, relationally—and then gotten up, dusted themselves off, and continued forward with the wisdom from that loss seared in both mind and heart. I would *never* follow a leader that is unbroken. He or she lacks the compassion and humility to lead others." This was not what the young executive expected or, quite frankly, accepted. He was looking for the magic bullet!

To lead is to engage others. In order to engage others, we must first be *fully engaged* ourselves. And the truth is that the seeds of consistent full engagement are forged in the moments that test us to the depth of our being. It is there that we learn what really matters and acquire the necessary humility to depend on God's great grace, rather than on our own inconsistent efforts.

Mark Batterson, pastor of National Community Church in Washington, DC, writes:

> When I'm going through a tough time emotionally or relationally or spiritually, I figure I'm getting an education in those areas. When it gets really tough, I think of it as graduate work. Everyone and everything become part of my education. God redeems them and uses them to shape me into the person He wants me to become.[36]

The examples of spectacular comebacks from failure or tragedy are inspiring to us:

- Albert Einstein was told by his math professor he would never amount to anything.
- Warren Buffett was rejected by the Harvard Business School.
- Steve Jobs was turned down by HP for an entry-level job and later fired by the company he founded—Apple.
- Juliette Magill Kinzie overcame the loss of her

hearing, her husband, and her home to found the Girl Scouts of the USA.

- Dan Luckett overcame a double amputation and is now one of 41 American amputees currently serving in combat zones.

Failure is not only an option— it's a prerequisite for living a *focused* life.

Before penning her best-selling Harry Potter series, J. K. Rowling was jobless and "as poor as it is possible to be in modern Britain, without being homeless." Looking back, she extols the essential benefits of adversity. "Failure meant the stripping away of the inessential. I stopped pretending to myself that I was anything other than who I was, and began to direct all my energy into finishing the only work that mattered to me."[37]

Stripping away the inessential allowed Rowling to DO *less* in order to BE *more*—in this case, to author a series of books that have become the fastest-selling books in history.

To be stripped of the inessential is often the first and necessary action step toward a *fully engaged* life. It empowers us to pursue what we are called to do.

In his book by the same title, Gene Kranz utters the famous phrase, "Failure is not an option," referring to bringing back the Apollo 13 astronauts alive. This may be true in successfully landing a space shuttle, or I suppose in skydiving, but it is perfectly wrong in leading a *focused* life. In fact, failure is not only an option—it's a prerequisite. I wish I could acquire the necessary education and consistent resolve to be *truly focused* in an easier, less painful way, but I truly don't know how.

Whether it's the loss of a job, financial failure, relational difficulty, or a spiritual dry spell, we are all faced with setbacks and difficulty. But by reflecting on our failures and mining these rich experiences for wisdom, we can move forward with a *fully engaged* life. So we might as well fail faster in order to engage sooner. In other words, step out. Risk falling flat. Take a leap of faith. How do you do that?

Across the back of our property, just west of Minneapolis, are a number of old-growth oak trees. They sway and bend in the raging winds of the fiercest thunderstorms but have never in the ten years we've lived here snapped under the pressure. It's said that "the greatest oak was once a little nut that held its ground." These majestic trees hold their ground, no matter what winds come their way.

Use the Defining Moments exercise on the next page to reflect on both the wins and losses of your life. Then focus on the setbacks as the crucial seeds for consistent actions that will allow you to hold your ground and lead to a *fully engaged* life.

Your engagement is fueled by failure. Where can you risk failing today?

DO *less*. BE *more*.

What Are Your Defining Moments?

On the life line below, record the Defining Moments you recall that have most impacted you. Place a dot below or above the line, rating them as neutral, high, or low points (*at the time*). The farther below the line they appear, the more negative they were, and the farther above the line they are, the more positive they were for you. Connect the dots with a line chronologically so you can clearly see your life's Defining Moments.

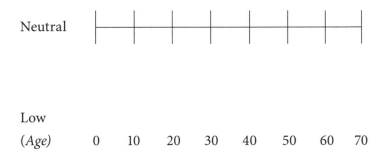

High

Neutral

Low

(*Age*)   0   10   20   30   40   50   60   70

What are the three setbacks that have most impacted your life?

1. _____

2. _____

3. _____

How do these Defining Moments impact your courage in *doing less* to *be more*?

CHAPTER EIGHT

Stay in Touch

You are designed to live in community.

The evening before setting out to climb Kilimanjaro, our young guide, Elias, gathered our party of 12 together for two critical tasks. First, he detailed the route we would be taking through five ecosystems, beginning in the Montane Forest with monkeys swinging in the trees and elephants foraging on the floor, culminating six days later on the glaciated summit of Kili. He wanted us to envision how we would feel and what we would see as the seven-day adventure unfolded. Elias also wanted to begin to build a relationship with each of us so he would know how best to lead our group.

The second, more important, task was to get our group to agree on how we would live together in community. Would we bond together and commit to summit as a group, or would we act as a collection of individuals who had all paid a healthy sum to get to Tanzania and felt entitled, no matter what happened, to stand on the highest peak on the African continent?

In the cozy confines of base camp, it seemed a no-brainer. We quickly agreed that if we didn't all summit together, no one would summit. All for one and one for all!

But by the fourth day of the adventure, our group had completely lost touch with each other. The distance between the first in our party to reach the afternoon camp and the last to stagger in was four hours! We had completely abandoned our covenant to hang together made only four days earlier. As Albert Einstein cautioned, "In theory, theory and practice are the same. In practice, they are not!" Out with the theory of community and in with the practice of the selfish pursuit of our own goals.

As was his ritual, Elias gathered us together at the end of the day to debrief and discuss the next day's journey. That fourth evening, he shared this sobering thought: "If you continue on tomorrow as you did today, some of you aren't going to make it."

He wasn't suggesting that somebody would die, but he was firm in his belief that to continue on as individuals would surely mean that a number of us wouldn't stand on the summit of Kili. Several in our party were already struggling with three days yet to go.

Right about this point in your journey toward a *fully engaged* life, you may look around and come to the shocking realization that you are alone in your pursuit because you've lost touch with others and even perhaps with yourself. There are two vital practices that serve the purpose of keeping us connected in our pursuit of a *fully engaged* life. The first is the discipline of daily reflection. The second is regular and courageous conversations with a Life Board that will accompany us on our journey.

Daily Reflection

A friend once shared with me that he was wrestling with a very important decision. "So," he said, "I spent the whole night in prayer."

Knowing my friend to be a Type A who usually is the smartest guy in the room and gets very quickly to the point, I asked somewhat incredulously, "All night? What could you possibly have to say that took *all night*?"

"I didn't say a word," he responded. "I just listened."

My friend was practicing the first discipline of staying connected—a quiet time of reflection and prayer. He was quieting his mind in order to discern the direction he should pursue in this critical decision. You see, clarity and creativity don't flow into a noisy mind. They come into a mind quieted from distraction and free of worry about yesterday and tomorrow.

In one of the most intimate descriptions in the Torah, Moses, a man tasked with leading the whole people of Israel, is seen meeting with God in this fashion:

> Now Moses used to take a tent and pitch it outside the camp some distance away, calling it the "tent of meeting." Anyone inquiring of the LORD would go to the tent of meeting outside the camp. And whenever

Moses went out to the tent, all the people rose and stood at the entrances to their tents, watching Moses until he entered the tent. The LORD would speak to Moses face to face, *as one speaks to a friend.*[38]

Clarity and creativity don't flow into a noisy mind. They come into a mind quieted from distraction and free of worry about yesterday and tomorrow.

As with every account in the Torah, there is more life wisdom here than initially meets the eye. Moses went "outside the camp" to meet with God. He removed himself from his routine and familiar surroundings to spend time face-to-face in quiet conversation.

The people he led waited in their tents in anxious expectation for Moses' return. Their experience was undoubtedly that he had something to say after his face time with God. Leaders who only read e-mail and hurry-scurry through their day ultimately have nothing impactful to say. They end up like Richard Foster's description of himself only three months into ministry:

My problem was more than having something to say from Sunday to Sunday. My problem was that what I did say had no power to help people. I had no substance, no depth. The people were starving for a word from God, and I had nothing to give them. Nothing. I was spiritually bankrupt and I knew it.[39]

In order to consistently live a *fully engaged* life, we need to set up our own "tent of meeting" outside the camp of our busy daily schedule and routines. The first, most important conversation at the beginning of each day is the inner conversation with ourselves and with God. We need to spelunk the inner caverns of our own heart and then ask for guidance and direction before we set out on our own to climb the summit of each day's journey.

Foster continues:

In contemporary society, our adversary majors in three things: noise, hurry, and crowds. If he can keep us engaged in "muchness" and "manyness," he will rest satisfied. Psychiatrist Carl Jung once remarked, "Hurry is not *of* the devil; it *is* the devil."

If we hope to move beyond the superficialities of our culture, including our religious culture, we must be willing to go down into the recreating silences, into the inner world of contemplation.[40]

We must develop the discipline to begin each day with a quiet time, free of distractions and noise, to seek out God's wisdom and counsel first before we step into the fray. This is *not* a technique or a to-do. It is a radical "one-on-one" time where we actively listen with the full intention of then obeying what we just heard.

Larry King starts each day with the reminder that "nothing I say this day will teach me anything. So, if I'm going to learn, I must do it by listening."

Beginning quietly empowers us to DO *less* of what are really periphery tasks and to BE *more* of who we are designed, called, and equipped to be. It allows us to move in from the marginal to the main events of the day. Days absent of reflection risk pursuit of false goals, squandered energy, overcommitment, and under fulfillment.

Life Board

We cannot let our reflection stay solely with us, however. We need to seek out the wise counsel and courageous accountability of others or we risk becoming legends in our own minds!

A Life Board is a strong support team. They are your own group of trusted people who offer support, counsel, and wisdom. Your Life Board members hold you accountable to living a *focused* life.

Your Life Board can include your spouse, partner, family members, colleagues, mentors, advisors, spiritual guides, and wise elders. The only thing they all have in common is you.

The core work of your Life Board is to engage, challenge, and inspire you. They provide you with feedback and resources to make sound choices and live *fully engaged*.

I have a "partial board meeting" every other Friday. I meet with a group of 10 men who have the perfect stories to be able to be present with each other in every life experience. We have been meeting for years—reading, praying, telling stories, and investing deeply in each other's lives. Speaking up with courage and transparency has opened the floodgates of reality. Once we set down the façade of lives lived in apparent order and daily calm and began to share the truth—the good, the bad, and the ugly about our work, relationships, faith, and family—we became a "band of brothers," knit together and able to inspire each other to live *focused* lives.

Over the last five years, jobs have been lost, health has wavered, relationships stumbled, and our faith has staggered—in other words, life has happened! And in every circumstance, there has been more than one man who has experienced, or was currently experiencing, exactly the same reality. Because of that, each of us has been able to gain new wisdom and perspective when we lacked it on our own.

We are also able to celebrate together the great wins promotions, graduations, grandchildren, and healings—and not think of each other as boastful or in any way self-sufficient or fiercely independent. We need each other.

All of this may sound quaint in an age of Twitter, Facebook, and IM-ing. Perhaps the more digital we become, the deeper our desire to spend at least part of our time in a very analog activity—speaking face-to-face "as one speaks to a friend" with God and with the vital people in our life. Maybe Moses convened the original and ultimate social-networking site!

If we are to live *focused* lives, we need to stay consistently in touch—with God, our self, and with a small group of intimate friends.

Use the exercise on the following page to build and engage your own Life Board. The result may be a small group of trusted advisors who are your own accountability partners for sharing your intimate reflections and commitments.

You are designed to live in community. Who are you connecting deeply with today?

DO *less.* BE *more.*

Your Life Board

Your Life Board members must all meet the following criteria:

- They're genuinely interested (versus interesting) in your life goals, values, and passions.
- They're specialists (versus generalists) that bring unique qualities that help you grow.
- They offer wisdom (versus information) in specific life dimensions.
- They're courageous (versus conciliatory), will be honest with you, and hold you to your commitments.

Selecting Your Life Board

Which three to five individuals fit the above criteria and might partner with you for the next year to help you achieve your goal of a *focused* life?

Friends or family members:

- _____
- _____
- _____

Mentors or guides:

- _____
- _____
- _____

Professional advisors or resources:

- _____
- _____
- _____

Wise elders and teachers:

- _____
- _____
- _____

Spiritual and community groups:

- _____
- _____
- _____

Roles of Your Life Board

Select the three to five people who will sit on your Life Board for the next year and identify the role you would like each of them to play. Roles might include listener, catalyst, specific wisdom, truth teller, support, accountability partner, etc.

Name: _____

Role: _____

Name: _____

Role: _____

Name: _____

Role: _____

Name: _____

Role: _____

Name: _____

Role: _____

CHAPTER NINE

Give It Away

Your engagement is sustained by generosity.

Early on in life, you probably learned the value of money. You discovered how much it took to buy an ice-cream cone and, much later, a car. Think for a minute about what you did with your first paycheck…and what you did with the paycheck you received last week. How you spend your money has everything to say not only about your priorities but also about your view of the world, your picture of yourself, and the value you place on others and your relationships.

Not long ago, there was an e-mail making the rounds that detailed the following cyclical rise and fall of all great civilizations:

From bondage to spiritual faith;
From spiritual faith to great courage;
From great courage to liberty;
From liberty to abundance;
From abundance to complacency;
From complacency to apathy;
From apathy to dependence;
From dependence back to bondage.

While the authorship of this theory may be in question, the progression makes perfect sense. And it applies not only to cultures but to personal life cycles as well. The critical point is *abundance*. What does a nation—or a person—do with abundance forged in freedom?

If you've been working through the practices at the end of each chapter, you may already be experiencing newfound abundance as a result of a *focused* life. Maybe you have more time because you are saying "No" more courageously to the peripheral and "Yes" more judiciously to the essential. Perhaps you have more energy to lavish on loved ones because your values are helping you focus on energy-giving versus energy-sapping activities, pursuits, and relationships.

Maybe your business is prospering with greater discipline and passion fueled by a sense of calling. Or perhaps your stress level is going down because you're not trying to do everything you used to.

The pivotal question is, what do you do with more time and energy?

The pivotal question is, what do you do with more time and energy?

Do you begin to take abundance for granted and find yourself slipping back to being enslaved by the tyranny of time and temptation to DO more? Or do you treat abundance as the open invitation to BE more generous than you ever thought possible?

Abundance awakens gratitude. Gratitude is the catalyst for generosity. And if the old adage is true—that it is more blessed to give than to receive—then generosity is at the very core of sustaining a *fully engaged* life.

I don't mean just giving a few extra minutes to a colleague or plunking a few bucks in the Salvation Army bucket outside the grocery store. I mean sacrificially giving fully of yourself to another person because you love them or dispensing dollars you don't even have to a person who needs them way more than you.

The progression of our life is determined by clearly answering these three questions that are the essence of generosity:

WHY give generously?
HOW give generously?
WHERE give generously?

Each question demands a bold, countercultural response that fuels an ever-growing practice of engagement.

WHY *give generously?*

The simple truth is that everything you have is a gift. Your ability to work, be in relationship with others, live, love, and prosper is ultimately fully dependent on your ability to breathe. And your daily breath is a gift.

There is no mystery to the rhythm of breathing: breathe in—breathe out—repeat. Hold your breath, and in minutes you're dead. You have to exhale to live.

The rhythm of life is the same: receive gifts—give gifts—repeat! To cling tenaciously to your stuff will kill you. The only thing you should collect is experiences. Everything else takes up space, requires maintenance, and can become a flashpoint of friction at death as siblings squabble over who gets what.

All of this flies in the face of the ruggedly individualistic, materialistic world in which we live, which speaks to us in the language of "It's yours. You've earned it. You own it. You can keep it. Retire on it. You can even control it beyond the grave if you plan well."

The people of Israel were cautioned against complacency as they stood on the threshold of an abundant life:

> GOD is about to bring you into a good land, a land
> with brooks and rivers, springs and lakes, streams

out of the hills and through the valleys. It's a land of wheat and barley, of vines and figs and pomegranates, of olives, oil, and honey. It's land where you'll never go hungry—always food on the table and a roof over your head. It's a land where you'll get iron out of rocks and mine copper from the hills.

If you start thinking to yourselves, "I did all this. And all by myself. I'm rich. It's all mine!"—well, think again. Remember that GOD, your God, gave you the strength to produce all this wealth.[41]

Your responsibility as a *fully engaged* friend, partner, colleague, parent, boss, spouse, sibling, and child is to regift your life!

Real generosity is never a campaign. It's a conspiracy. It conspires to move us from the poverty of *seeking more* to an abundance of *enjoying enough*. It challenges our instinct to *selfishly grasp* with a command to *sacrificially give*. Generosity transforms our worldview from being *outwardly driven to distraction* to being *inwardly called to contentment*. It summons us to move beyond building a *lifestyle* to leaving a lasting *legacy*. In the end, it is rocket fuel for a *fully engaged* life. But it also requires a radical reframing of our self-dependent point of view.

Real generosity is never a campaign. It's a conspiracy.

In the mid-'80s, only 15 percent of Americans wore seat belts. The government tried to mandate usage, but in spite of the obvious safety benefits, people resisted the change as "big government intervention." Only after the issue was recast as a means of protecting children did people begin to wear seat belts. Three years later, 80 percent of Americans were wearing them, usually as a response to the question "Mommy, how come I'm wearing a seat belt and you're not?" Reframing the issue brought about a change in behavior and law.

When we reframe generosity from an obligation or a mandate to the natural response to being richly blessed with gifts we truly haven't earned, giving sacrificially is the powerful outcome.

To remain *fully engaged*, we must be "Sea of Galilee" people.

> The Sea of Galilee has an outlet. It gets to give. It gathers in its riches that it may pour them out again

to fertilize the Jordan Plain. But the Dead Sea with the same water makes horror. For the Dead Sea has no outlet. It gets to keep.[42]

Why give? Because you have received. You get to give. Breathe in—breathe out—repeat!

HOW *give generously?*

Generosity is a lifelong process of growing up. With money, what may start as a sporadic gift to a person in need may progress to occasional checks, a pledge, or even a tithe to a local place of worship. But eventually we are confronted with the piercing question: "Do we truly love our neighbor as ourselves?" Real generosity begins where giving leaves off. It involves the sacrifice of something of great value for the good of another.

Actor Paul Newman's breakthrough came when James Dean, who was cast as the leading man for a 1956 film about the boxer Rocky Graziano, was killed in a car crash. The film was titled *Somebody Up There Likes Me.* Newman agreed, and he lived his life from that point forward as if somebody really did.

With an Academy Award for best actor, film-directing success, a 50-year marriage, and racing autos into his late

70s, few would question whether Newman lived a *fully engaged* life. In the end, it was his generosity more than his acting that distinguished his life:

> His sauces and snacks, sold for charity from 1982 onwards ("shameless exploitation in pursuit of the common good") turned him into the most generous individual, relative to his income, in the 20th century history of the United States.[43]

To date, his Newman's Own brand has generated more than $300 million for charitable causes around the world, of which his favorite were his 11 Hole in the Wall Camps for children with life-threatening illnesses.

Somebody "up there" likes you, too. As a matter of fact, He LOVES you! The most powerful response to His love is crazy generosity, and in so doing, sustaining a *fully engaged* life of service to others.

How do you give? The words of Swedish author and diplomat Dag Hammarskjöld give us a wonderful glimpse into the *how* of a generous life: "For all that has been: Thanks. For all that shall be: Yes."

Yes is the practice field of generosity.

Yes to viewing your life as far greater than money.

Yes to sharing your story and courageously living your values.

Yes to working out of a sense of calling.

Yes to dreaming big and being fully present.

Yes to embracing setbacks as steps forward.

Yes to nutritious relationships.

And finally, *Yes* to giving generously of yourself.

WHERE give generously?

With 12 months, 52 weeks, 365 days, 78,760 hours, and 525,600 minutes in this next year, where do you sacrificially give your *truly focused* life? And then, what about the next year? And the one after that?

Our son Josh writes of his deep experience of generosity in South Africa:

> While sharing, hope, survival, love, and kindness are clearly not new ideals for me, I have never seen them acted out in daily life as fully as Kwanele embraces them. Kwanele has lived a tough life for someone who is only six years old. He was abandoned by his father, is HIV positive, only has one lung due to TB, and has other health issues that have an impact on his daily routine.

Despite the hardships he has had to endure, Kwanele could quite possibly be the happiest (and cutest) kid I have ever seen. My heart melts a little bit each week that I am at the orphanage and Kwanele provides me with a model of how to live in a God-loving manner.

Just last week, I made the trek up to a store a few meters from the orphanage to purchase *ma guina* (deep fried dough—it's quite delicious really!). The first kid I saw upon my return was Kwanele, so I gave him a piece of the cake. While I was breaking off a piece for one of the other boys, Kwanele beat me to the punch by breaking his piece in half and giving it to a boy next to him.

While this might seem like a small gesture, think about it a little deeper with me. Here is a boy who eats only a few bites a day and rarely gets a treat like a fat cake. Yet before even taking a bite of the piece I gave him, he is ready to make his portion smaller so another boy can savor the moment with him.

Where do you give? It may begin with the person sitting right next to you and radiate from there out to the world. Your dreams "borne out of a burden" from chapter 5 contain the seedbed for where to be generous with your *fully engaged* life. Use The Generous Life exercise on the following page to turn one of your dreams into a powerful expression of generosity in the next year. The result may be the continued expansion of your *fully engaged* life, fueled by a deep sense of gratitude.

Your engagement is sustained by generosity. What are you giving away today?

DO *less*. BE *more*.

The Generous Life

WHERE give generously? (What Life Dream do I lavish with generosity?)

_____

WHY give generously? (What values does this serve?)

_____

WHO will support me? (Which Life Board members will give me support and hold me accountable?)

_____

HOW will I give? (What are my milestones toward accomplishment?)

1. _____

DUE DATE _____ ☐

2. _____

DUE DATE _____ ☐

3. _____

DUE DATE _____ ☐

4. _____

DUE DATE _____ ☐

5. _____

DUE DATE _____ ☐

WHAT are the tradeoffs?

_____

_____

_____

HOW will I celebrate?

_____

_____

_____

DO Less to BE More

You can choose to live purposefully.

On August 24, 2006, 2,500 scientists meeting in Prague made it official: Pluto isn't what it used to be—at least it isn't what it had been for the previous 75 years—a planet. With its small size and oddball orbit, scientists had long argued that it should never have been deemed a planet in the first place.

Listening the next day to an astronomer discuss the landmark decision on National Public Radio, I heard an outpouring of emotion—from raw anger to dismay to sadness. Adults and children alike had become accustomed to a particular view of the solar system that included the ninth planet, Pluto.

Caller after caller asked some version of the question, "How could this be? How could the solar system include nine planets yesterday and only eight today?"

"What will I tell my children?" one woman asked. It was as if people felt a need to stick up for the poor little underdog planet, Pluto.

Mike Brown, a professor at Caltech, was the man who inadvertently caused this interplanetary crisis when he discovered Eris, an object even farther from the sun than Pluto but considerably more massive. He went on to write a book about his discovery: *How I Killed Pluto and Why It Had It Coming.*

Science is changing. Continuous discovery and technological advances alter what was just yesterday treated as fact and fixed in stone.

Hopefully, this book has caused you to change some of the views to which you had perhaps become accustomed as well. To alter your health routine, work rhythm, study habits, generosity, or relationship pattern is difficult. You can become accustomed to your own groove. Over time, your groove deepens into a rut, and you can get buried alive. The difference between a rut and a grave is merely the depth of the excavation. To re-cut any rut is a lot of work. To escape a grave is miraculous.

Look at fitness, for example. Of 100 people who join a health club, seven never go at all. Twenty-five percent quit in the first month. Seventy-five percent quit in the first three months. So, of the original 100, only 17 remain after just three months.[44] And sculpting our abs or firming up our butt is a superficial change. It's an outside job.

Living a *fully engaged* life is an inside job requiring you to change some core beliefs and long-accepted practices. It demands that you DO *less* in order for you to BE *more*.

It's going to require courage and resolve to pursue a *fully engaged* life. Such a change is seldom convenient and often counterintuitive. It certainly will fly in the face of "conventional wisdom." To follow through on your discoveries and commitments will require sacrifice, discipline, and tenacity.

Don't wait, procrastinate, hesitate, or deliberate. Boldly choosing to make good on all of the talents and promise you were born with—to live purposefully beginning today—empowers you to enjoy the satisfaction, success, and excitement that comes with a *focused* life.

It will allow you to move beneath the surface of things and find great significance and deep fulfillment in your everyday life.

I wish you rich blessings as you choose to DO *less* in order to BE *more*!

Tell me, what is it you plan to do
with your one wild and precious life?
—MARY OLIVER, *The Summer Day*

FOCUS POINTS

What's the ONE thing?

Use the following **FOCUS POINTS** to zero in
on one action you commit to taking as a result of
reading each chapter of *do less, be more*.

1. Measure your worth—Which single Life-dimension, if strengthened or grown, would have the biggest impact over the other nine dimensions? **GROW IT**

_____

_____

_____

_____

_____

_____

_____

_____

_____

_____

_____

_____

_____

_____

_____

2. Share your story—Given the opportunity, what's the one question you'd love to ask your parents? **ASK IT**

_____

_____

_____

_____

_____

_____

_____

_____

_____

_____

_____

_____

_____

_____

_____

_____

_____

_____

3. Do what matters—What is the top value that you'd like to show up in your calendar? **LIVE IT**

_____

_____

_____

_____

_____

_____

_____

_____

_____

_____

_____

_____

_____

_____

_____

_____

_____

4. Occupy your space—What is the #1 strength that fuels your calling? **USE IT**

_____

_____

_____

_____

_____

_____

_____

_____

_____

_____

_____

_____

_____

_____

_____

_____

5. Dream wide awake—What's tops on your Life-Dream list? **START IT**

6. Drop the ball—What is the distraction that causes you to be unfocused most frequently? **STOP IT**

7. Celebrate your setbacks—What failure has been the most influential to your success? **LEVERAGE IT**

8. Stay in touch—What is your best method for connecting deeply with others? **PRACTICE IT**

_____

_____

_____

_____

_____

_____

_____

_____

_____

_____

_____

_____

_____

_____

9. Give it away—What is the one thing, which if given away, would unleash a flood of new generosity? **GIVE IT**

Life Worth Satisfaction Scoring:

40–50: Congratulations! You are living a *fully engaged* life. Continue to monitor and invest in your most valued life dimensions.

25–39: You are in positive territory with your engagement. With some systematic attention to valued life dimensions, you could significantly increase your ability to enjoy a *fully engaged* life. DO *less*. BE *more*.

10–24: You are somewhat disengaged with your life. Where can you invest time and energy in order to increase your satisfaction with living a *fully engaged* life? What balls do you need to drop? DO *less*. BE *more*!

0–9: You are dangerously disengaged! Take time NOW to review your life dimensions. Drop some balls and quickly begin to invest in the dimensions that matter most to you. You are designed to BE *more*. WAY *more*!

ACKNOWLEDGMENTS

To Brett—our great son who continues to inspire and help me live a focused life as I gracefully age!

To Josh—our other great son who continuously models a generous and free-spirited life.

To Mallory—for saying yes to becoming an "official" part of our family and being the daughter we never had until now.

To the Friday guy's group—for being an Acts 2 Church for 10 years and an inspiring source of love, life and laughter every other week.

To Kent—your love and inspiration started this journey 6 years ago and you continue to be "Exhibit A" of a focused and faithful life.

To Jason—you stuck with *Fully Engaged* and introduced me to the wonderfully creative team at Freeman-Smith.

To Ramona—for your clarifying question that launched this book and amazing ability to turn my scribbling into a wonderful narrative.

To Paul—my dear friend and encourager, for lending the tender story of your dad and for challenging me to always raise my writing game.

To Steve—my coffee buddy and tireless encourager, for your prayers, deep faith, stories and ever-persistent push to hammer away at this project.

To Dave—whose unvarnished input has provoked belly laughs and whose divine teaching has caused my faith to grow more in a year than the previous twenty-five.

To Joel—who allowed me to test drive many of these concepts for years and whose friendship has been a remarkable blessing for almost 30 years.

To Brad—you are blessing me by radically expanding my view and practice of what it is to be truly generous.

And to my mom and dad – for loving me enough to start me on my faith journey when I was a little boy and for still praying for me daily today.

Endnotes

[1] Os Guinness, *The Call* (Nashville, TN: Thomas Nelson, Inc., 2003), italics added, 4.

[2] Po Bronson, "What Should I Do with My Life?" *Fast Company,* December 19, 2007.

[3] Luke 12:22–24, italics added.

[4] Robert Dickman, "The Four Elements of Every Successful Story," http://www.storyatwork.com/documents/4Elements ofStory_BobDickman.pdf.

[5] Krista Tippett, "Rules for Discussing the Meaning of It All," *WSJ,* November 20–21, 2010.

[6] David McCullough, "April 18, 2005: Knowing History and Knowing Who We Are," from talk February 15, 2005, in Phoenix, Arizona, at a Hillsdale College National Leadership Seminar on the topic "American History and America's Future," http://www.realclearpolitics.com/Commentary/com-4_18_05_ DM.html.

[7] MSNBC.com, "Miracle on the Hudson: All Safe in Jet Crash," January 15, 2009; http://www.msnbc.msn.com/id/28678669/ns/ us_news-life/.

[8] Jeffrey Zaslow, "What We Can Learn from Sully's Journey," *The Wall Street Journal,* October 14, 2009, http://online.wsj.com/article/SB10001424052748703790404574469160016077646.html.

[9] "Discovering Your Authentic Leadership," *Harvard Business Review,* February, 2007.

[10] Luke 16:10–14.

[11] John Ortberg, "Tiger and the Good Life," LeadershipJournal. net, www.ChristianityToday.com, December 14, 2009, http:// www.christianitytoday.com/le/currenttrendscolumns/leader-shipweekly/tigerandthegoodlife.html.

[12] William Guth and Renato Tagiuri, "Personal Values and Corporate Strategy," *Harvard Business Review*, September–October 1965.

[13] Richard Leider, "Go to Hell Money," *Fast Company,* April 2000, italics added.

[14] Alice Woodmark.

[15] John Ortberg, "Ministry and FTT," LeadershipJournal.net, posted 6/09/2008, www.ChristianityToday.com, http://www.christianitytoday.com/le/currenttrendscolumns/leadershipweekly/cln80609.html.

[16] Po Bronson, *What Should I Do With My Life?* (New York: Simon & Schuster, 2003).

[17] Isak Dinesen, *Out of Africa* (New York: Modern Library/ Random House, Inc., 1992), 4.

[18] Galatians 6:4–5.

[19] Frederick Buechner, *Wishful Thinking: A Seeker's ABC* (San Francisco: Harper San Francisco, 1993).

[20] Saint Francis de Sales (1567–1622).

[21] Jonathan Goddard in "Taking Charge," The Inventure Group, 93.

[22] 1 Kings 3:5 NIV, italics added.

[23] 1 Kings 3:9, italics added.

[24] John Ortberg, *The Me I Want to Be* (Grand Rapids, Mich.: Zondervan, 2009).

[25] For more information, http://www.onedayswages.org.

[26] Mark Batterson, "Don't Take Yes for an Answer," from *Primal: A Quest for the Lost Soul of Christianity* (Colorado Springs, CO: The Waterbrook Multnomah Publishing Group, 2009).

[27] "Seeing the Water," by Matt Tebbe, LeadershipJournal.net, posted 10/4/2010, www.christianitytoday.com, http://www.christianitytoday.com/le/currenttrendscolumns/bookreviews/seeingwater.html.

[28] Martin Schmutterer, "This is your brain…This is your brain on the Internet," *Star Tribune* (Minneapolis, Minn.), June 27, 2010, http://www.startribune.com/entertainment/books/97182029.html.

[29] Christine Rosen, "Can You Finish This Story without Being Interrupted?" thestar.com, posted July 2, 2008, http://www.thestar.com/living/article/452322.

[30] *Wall Street Journal*, September 12, 2006.

[31] Kermit Pattison, "Worker, Interrupted: The Cost of Task Switching," *Fast Company,* July 28, 2008, http://www.fastcompany.com/articles/2008/07/interview-gloria-mark.html.

[32] Martha Coventry, "Slow Down Your Life."

[33] Richard J. Foster, *Freedom of Simplicity: Finding Harmony in a Complex World* (San Francisco: HarperOne, 2005).

[34] Richard J. Foster, *Celebration of Discipline: The Path to Spiritual Growth* (San Francisco: HarperOne, 1998), 1.

[35] Pat Conroy, *My Losing Season: A Memoir* (New York: Random House, Inc., 2003).

[36] Mark Batterson, *Don't Take Yes for an Answer.*

[37] Eliza Sarasohn, "The Right Way to Fail," *Experience Life* magazine, January/February, 2010, http://www.experiencelifemag.com/issues/january-february-2010/life-wisdom/the-right-way-to-fail.php.

[38] Exodus 33:7–8, 11 NIV, italics added for paraphrase.

[39] Richard J. Foster, *Celebration of Discipline,* xiii.

[40] Richard J. Foster, *Celebration of Discipline,* 15.

[41] Deuteronomy 8:7–9, 17.

[42] Henry Emerson Fosdick (1878–1969).

[43] Obituary, Paul Newman, *The Economist,* October 4, 2008.

[44] Columbia University.

About the Author

John Busacker is president of INVENTURE, a global leadership-consulting firm, and founder of *Life*-Worth, LLC, a pioneer in holistic financial advice. He is a member of the Duke Corporate Education Global Learning Resource Network and is on the faculty of the University of Minnesota Carlson School's Executive Development Center.

His travels have taken him to six continents to work with leading organizations such as Medtronic, CJ Corporation of South Korea, Ameriprise, Pricewaterhouse Coopers, the Good Samaritan Foundation, Thrivent Financial, the Mayo Clinic, Boston Children's Hospital Trust, the Mohammed Bin Rashid Programme for Leadership Development, Calvert Investments, and The Pastoral Leadership Institute International.

John released his first book, *8 Questions God Can't Answer*, which unlocks the profound power of Jesus' timeless questions, in 2009. He annually teaches in a variety of emerging faith communities and supports the development needs of indigenous leaders through PLI-International.

John is the author of *Life-Based Financial Planning*™, a leading-edge system for aligning finances with life values and personal purpose, and architect of STEWARD*shift*™, an innovative guide to generous living. As a commentator on life/work issues, John has written for or been cited in *The Wall Street Journal, Los Angeles Times,* Minneapolis *Star Tribune, Research* magazine, and *Experience Life* magazine.

John is an avid explorer, occasional marathoner, and novice cyclist. He and his wife, Carol, live in Minneapolis and have two adult sons, Brett and Joshua.

dolessandbemore.com | www.inventuregroup.com